Free Trade Today

Free Trade Today

Jagdish Bhagwati

PRINCETON UNIVERSITY PRESS

Princeton and Oxford

Published by Princeton University Press, 41 William Street,
Princeton, New Jersey 08540
In the United Kingdom: Princeton University Press, 3 Market Place,
Woodstock, Oxfordshire OX20 1SY

LIBRARY OF CONGRESS CATALOGING-IN-PUBLICATION DATA
Bhagwati, Jagdish N., 1934–
Free trade today / Jagdish Bhagwati.
p. cm.
Includes bibliographical references and index.
ISBN 0-691-09156-0
1. Free trade. 2. Free trade—Environmental aspects. 3. Free trade—
Social aspects. 4. Free trade—United States. 5. International
economic relations. I. Title.
HF1713 .B465 2002
382′.71—dc21   2001036913

British Library Cataloging-in-Publication Data is available

This book has been composed in Minion

Printed on acid-free paper. ∞

www.pup.princeton.edu

Printed in the United States of America

1 3 5 7 9 10 8 6 4 2

Contents

Preface

IN 1987, I was invited to give the first Bertil Ohlin Lectures at the Stockholm School of Economics, leading to the publication of *Protectionism* (1988) by MIT Press. The lectures were widely reviewed and read, even translated into several languages.

A decade later, I gave three lectures collectively titled "Free Trade Today," again at the Stockholm School of Economics. By the 1990s, the opposition facing the proponents of free trade had changed dramatically. I myself engaged in many public debates, both face-to-face, as when I took on Ralph Nader in the Town Hall of Seattle in November 1999 (when the World Trade Organization Ministerial failed amid chaos) in the presence of literally hundreds of his electrically charged followers, and in invited lectures worldwide and op-ed articles in innumerable magazines and newspapers. Videotapes exist of the debates, and my public-policy writings in the popular media and elsewhere have been collected in two volumes also published by MIT Press: *A Stream of Windows: Unsettling Reflections on Trade, Immigration, and Democracy* (1998) and *The Wind of the Hundred Days: How Washington Mismanaged Globalization* (2001).

But what is needed is a sequel to *Protectionism,* an equally short, accessible, wide-ranging work that brings the case for free trade to the skeptics and the critics today, indeed to every citizen as she encounters the confrontations over free trade and must decide who is right. Engaging in this argument is essential to the only kind of democracy that is worth having: a deliberative democracy.

This need also imposes an obligation on scholars such as myself. We must certainly remain at the frontiers of science, but we must also go to the arena where policy is made, be engaged so that policy is improved. And we must ensure that our writings and debates on policy reflect our best science. When we write such pieces, they must be, not the froth of an afternoon required by a newspaper contract to write on demand, but built on a foundation of scholarship.

This is what I have hoped to accomplish in these lectures. They provide a panoramic view of postwar developments in the theory of free trade, drawing out the key insights that have revolutionized the (favorable) way we think about free trade. These ideas reflect much of my own work, an indulgence permitted by my being at the lectern but also required because economics is done best when, like literature, it reflects one's own experience. But I weave these theoretical insights into the policy issues, both old and new, in a way that shows, I hope, the creative relationship between the ivory tower and the world outside.

No scholar, no engaged intellectual, can be without debts. So I must acknowledge that I have learned much from my students and friends, too numerous to list all, over more than forty years of academic life. I should particularly like to recall, however, my students Gene Grossman, Paul Krugman, Robert Feenstra, Richard Brecher, Donald Davis, Douglas Irwin, Magnus Blomström, Elias Dinopoulos, Karyiu Wong, and Vivek Dehejia; and my friends Avinash Dixit, Elhanan Helpman, Robert Baldwin, Kyle Bagwell, Robert Staiger, T. N. Srinivasan, Assar Lindbeck, Arvind Panagariya, Alan Deardorff, and Robert Stern.

I have profited (though I use that word mischievously since it is anathema to those I thank now) also from arguing with Ralph Nader and Lori Wallach; and from working or talking with civil-society activists, especially those—chief among them Pradeep Mehta and Martin Khor—from the developing countries, whose perspectives and concerns are often ignored by nongovernmental groups and by the media in the rich countries. These individuals have provided perspectives that have enabled me to write more meaningfully about today's antitrade arguments.

The secretarial and research assistance provided by Olivia Carballo, Maria Coppola, and Bikas Joshi has been very helpful. The facilities provided by the Council on Foreign Relations, New York, where I am currently the André Meyer Senior Fellow in International Economics, have been most congenial; I owe special thanks to Leslie Gelb, Lawrence Korb, and Theophilos Gemelas. Thanks also are due to Magnus Bloström and Assar Lindbeck for inviting me to give these lectures.

Free Trade Today

Confronting Conventional Threats to Free Trade: The Postwar Revolution in the Theory of Commercial Policy

Why Free Trade Fails to Persuade

Conventional Dissent from Within:
Key Role of Market Failure or Distortions

Returning to Free Trade:
Fixing Domestic Distortions Directly

Tackling External Distortions:
Restoring Free Trade Differently

Theory of Directly Unproductive Profit-Seeking Activities:
Reinforcing the Case for Free Trade

Free Trade and Growth

THE merit of free trade was discovered and disclosed by Adam Smith in his monumental work *The Wealth of Nations* (though, as with Newton and Leibniz on calculus, we must recognize the remarkable work of Abbé de Condillac, whose essay *Commerce and Government* was published in the same year as *The Wealth of Nations* and is a far more elegant and sharp statement of this case).[1] The rationale for free trade is thus over two centuries old. Building his case on the gains from trade to be had from specialization reflecting the division of labor, Smith had the essence of the argument right. But it was left to David Ricardo (building on James Mill) to clinch the case formally. Ricardo used a stripped-down model—only one factor of production with constant productivity of

[1] *Commerce and Government* is now available in a splendid translation by the historian Shelagh Eltis. Cf. Etienne Bonnot, abbé de Condillac, *Commerce and Government*, with introduction by Shelagh and Walter Eltis (Cheltenham, U.K.: Edward Elgar, 1997). Interestingly, Condillac was also a philosopher of the French Enlightenment.

The contrasting styles of Adam Smith and Abbé de Condillac remind one of Marshall set against Walras. Thus, for instance, as the vast scholarship on Smith has variously demonstrated, his more discursive style and work sets out several "practical" exceptions to the case for free trade, and to the larger case for laissez-faire. See, for instance, Jacob Viner's essay "Adam Smith and Laissez Faire," reprinted in his *Essays on the Intellectual History of Economics*, ed. Douglas Irwin (Princeton: Princeton University Press, 1991), 85–113.

labor in two goods, but with relative productivity between the goods different across two countries—to show that both countries could gain from trade via specialization.[2] The Ricardian analysis implied that this "technical possibility" of gaining from trade would be realized if a policy of free trade were adopted in an institutional setting where prices guided resource allocation. But the analytically satisfactory proofs of trade's benefits that we modern economists demand are the handiwork of theorists working in the twentieth century.[3]

[2] Thus, I have argued since my "Survey of the Pure Theory of International Trade," *Economic Journal* 74 (1964): 1–26, that the interpretation of the Ricardian analysis, not in normative terms, but as a positive theory of comparative advantage explaining the pattern of trade, is not meaningful if one reads Ricardo in the original and sees that, when it came to positive analysis, he and other classical economists deployed a more complex and fuller-bodied model as in their analysis of the approach of the stationary state. Yet, of course, that is how many trade economists continue to this day to interpret it.

[3] In particular, after the early work of Paul Samuelson in 1939, he and Murray Kemp took important steps in mid-1950s towards demonstrating that free trade was Pareto-superior to autarky in static analysis. Cf. Paul Samuelson, "The Gains from International Trade Once Again," *Economic Journal* 72 (1962): 820–29; and Murray Kemp, "The Gains from International Trade," *Economic Journal* 72 (1972): 803–19.

The complete proof of the static gains from trade was finally provided by Jean Michel Grandmont and Daniel McFadden, "A Technical Note on Classical Gains from Trade," *Journal of International Economics* 2 (1972): 109–25. The extension of the case for free trade in an intertemporal setting owes to several authors, chief among them Torsten Persson and Alan Stockman, Avinash Dixit and Paul Samuelson. Questions relating to trade, growth, and welfare raise a separate set of issues that are touched upon later in this lecture.

Why Free Trade Fails to Persuade

But if the heuristically quite persuasive (and for its time even scientifically compelling) Smith-Ricardo demonstration of the gains from trade via specialization and the associated case for free trade was to win approval from a majority of economists in nearly every generation since the publication of *The Wealth of Nations*, it is also a fact that it has only infrequently carried credibility with the populace at large. Why?

Part of the reason has to do with the counterintuitive nature of the argument that free trade leads to greater good. When asked by the mathematician Stanislaw Ulam (the brother of the great historian Adam Ulam) which proposition in the social sciences was the most counterintuitive yet compelling, Paul Samuelson chose the law of comparative advantage: in other words, the underlying argument for free trade. Most people think it intuitively sound that you should do most things that you do better than others, not specialize. Then again, they seem to attach an infinite weight to jobs that they lose to trade and zero weight to jobs that are created and which they might obtain, in an optical illusion that reflects the way some experimental psychologists think we think when confronted with change.

Today, however, free trade is the target of a growing anticapitalist and antiglobalization agitation among the young that derives from what I like to call the *tyranny of the missing alternative*. The collapse of communism, the ideological system that rivaled capitalism, and the rise of Fukuyama-led triumphalism about markets and capitalism[4] have created

---

[4] Cf. Francis Fukuyama, *The Last Man* (New York: Free Press, 1990).

an intolerable void among the idealist young whose social conscience is attuned to the conviction that capitalism is a source of injustice. They do not see that capitalism can destroy privilege and open up economic opportunity to the many. I wonder how many of them are aware that Mrs. Thatcher was a grocer's daughter and that, with all her failings, her leadership of the Conservative Party saw the rise to high levels of many who had, not a BBC accent or an inherited title, but simply merit. How many understand that socialist planning in countries like India, aimed at replacing markets with quantitative allocations, often accentuated, instead of reducing, unequal access because the latter meant queues that the well-connected and well-endowed could jump with their moneys, whereas the former allowed a larger number to get to the desired targets?[5] The untutored conviction that markets and capitalism are to be equated with social injustice has fueled the frustration that spills over into the street theater staged against free trade and its principal institution, the World Trade Organization.

Then again, many students in literature and sociology in the English-speaking world on both sides of the Atlantic have been captivated and captured by the poststructural deconstructionism associated with the French philosopher

[5] This paradoxical conclusion was reached by me and Padma Desai in our book *India: Planning for Industrialization* (Oxford: Oxford University Press, 1970) in the OECD project directed by Ian Little, Tibor Scitovsky, and Maurice Scott. This conclusion has been reached also by many other empirical analysts of trade and industrialization policies in the developing countries.

Jacques Derrida, leaving many among them, principally because of its advocacy of an "endless horizon of meanings," without any anchor. As Terry Eagleton, the sympathetic chronicler of modern developments in literary theory, has said eloquently:[6] "Derrida is clearly out to do more than develop new techniques of reading: deconstruction is for him an ultimately *political* practice, an attempt to dismantle the logic by which a particular system of thought, and behind that a whole system of political structures and social institutions, maintains its force." By deconstructing any political ideology, the Derridean technique can lay before itself a political wasteland where belief and action yield to cynicism and anarchism. This leads equally to the paradox that a highly intellectual theory feeds anti-intellectual attitudes, including a distrust of, and hostility to, economic expertise and the "elitism" of economists.

Permit me to tell just three anecdotes to illustrate what I mean. In a debate at the Smithsonian Institute in Washington, D.C., that I had with Lori Wallach, an architect of the Seattle protests and Ralph Nader's chief aide on trade issues, she argued that my expertise on trade entitled me to no more attention by the GATT (General Agreement on Tariffs and Trade) or the WTO than she demanded for herself.

I must also recall that Sylvia Nasar, the former *New York Times* economics reporter, once told me that students in her class at the Columbia School of Journalism had told her that "Bhagwati stands for special interests as much as the unions

---

[6] Terry Eagleton, *Literary Theory: An Introduction* (Oxford: Basil Blackwell, 1983), 148.

do; he speaks for free trade and for the GATT." In short, we economists may profess expertise; but we really serve masters and interests that can be deconstructed from our arguments and advocacy.

Then again, I should retell the amusing story of how militant students at Heidelberg during the years of the Vietnam War declared that expertise was the enemy of genuine democracy and argued that democracy therefore required that professors teach courses that they knew nothing about, so that they and the students could start with equal ignorance, and hence without unequal power, on their journey towards knowledge. I must confess that I would have opted for this brilliant suggestion. It would mean that I would not have to exert myself to harness my knowledge to lecture to my students, so that I would be on perpetual sabbatical, something that some of my tenured colleagues (who must naturally remain unnamed) have been enjoying for years without the benefit of the Heidelberg doctrine!

But let me say also that the case for free trade in the public domain has suffered from neglect because few of us have been prepared to enter the fray in its defense. Faced with the critics of free trade, economists have generally reacted with contempt and indifference, refusing to get into the public arena to engage the critics in battle. I was in a public debate with Ralph Nader on the campus of Cornell University a couple of years ago. The debate was in the evening, and in the afternoon I gave a technical talk on free trade to the graduate students of economics. I asked, at its end, how many were going to the debate, and not one hand went up. Why, I asked. The typical reaction was: why waste one's time? As a consequence, of the nearly thousand students who jammed the theater where the debate was held, the vast majority were anti–free traders, all rooting for Mr. Nader. I managed pretty well, but I must confess that the episode brought home to me that unless we confront these misguided critics, the public-policy stage will be occupied solely by the critics of free trade, and then politicians cannot be blamed for having to listen and attend to the chorus of free trade's critics.

This task of ceaselessly defending our scientific findings in favor of free trade (and indeed of other economic wisdom) is an obligation that I teach tirelessly to my students, not just in emulation of their teacher, but in exercise of their own talents and conscience. Thus, among them, I must cite in particular the distinguished writings in the media of Paul Krugman (my remarkable MIT student) and Douglas Irwin (my gifted Columbia student).[7] But that is still not an army

---

[7] Among the friends and coauthors who write frequently on trade policy are Arvind Panagariya of Maryland, T. N. Srinivasan of Yale, Dani Rodrik of the Kennedy School, Harvard, and Robert Baldwin of Wisconsin, all world-class trade economists. After the Seattle debacle in late 2000, I and other international trade economists felt the need to start an ongoing group of trade scholars at universities that would enter the policy scene with policy briefs and multisignature statements on important policy issues of the day. Such a group, ACIT (the Academic Consortium on International Trade), has now been formed and is housed at the University of Michigan under the active leadership of the distinguished trade economists Robert Stern and Alan Deardorff. Its first piece of activism was the issuance of a letter to presidents of U.S. colleges and universities on the issues raised by the campus activism against sweatshops regarding the

that, unlike Russell Crowe in the film *Gladiator* with his Roman legions, I can "command" and that we need.

When I was at Seattle and facing a tough Chinese Red Guards–style female demonstrator who was blocking my way illegally down a road and threatening me with bodily harm if I persisted, my good friend Gary Sampson (a distinguished trade economist, formerly of the GATT and WTO) drew me away from a confrontation that would have surely left me bloodied, saying, "You are the foremost free trader today; we cannot afford to lose you!" It was meant to be funny, and it was. But it also was a pointed reference that there were not too many of us out there, fighting the fight for free trade. We need to change that.

I would be remiss, however, if I do not also record here the *fallacy of aggregation* that has made large segments of the public today gratuitously more skeptical of free trade worldwide thanks illogically to the dramatic recent financial crises in the world economy. For reasons that are difficult to fathom, the antiglobalization agitationists seem to think that globalization is some sort of gigantic blob of a concept or phenomenon where every element necessarily implies every other and that if you are for free trade, you must also be for free short-term capital flows, for free direct foreign investment, for free immigration, for free love, for free whatever![8]

---

suppliers of apparel to these academic institutions, arguing that the presidents were often succumbing to agitationist demands without informed analysis of the issues involved.

[8] I have dealt with the fallacy of aggregation and a number of other fallacies that feed today's antiglobalization rhetoric and agitation in my

So, if the imprudently hasty and unregulated freeing of financial flows helped create the panic-fed Asian financial crisis, then somehow that is also a reason to dread and to oppose freer trade. Indeed, *any* substantial international financial crisis, in this way of seeing things, is an argument against freer trade. Thus, the American critics of NAFTA (North American Free Trade Agreement) have pointed to the November 1994 peso crisis as justifying their hostility to NAFTA. Similarly, I have been surprised that even sophisticated economists who are distrustful of globalization, such as Dani Rodrik of Harvard, have occasionally argued as if the need to fix the world financial system because of recurring financial crises implies also that the world trade system needs to be fixed.[9]

Conventional Dissent from Within: Key Role of Market Failure or Distortions

But it would be a big mistake to think that the case for free trade has been assailed by doubts only from outside the sanctum. Indeed, from Adam Smith's time, major economists have abandoned the cause of free trade, reflecting in-

review-essay "Globalization in Your Face," *Foreign Affairs* 79, no. 4 (2000): 134–39.

[9] Cf. Dani Rodrik, "The Global Fix," *New Republic*, November 2, 1998; and my letter to the editor, critiquing the article, on December 14, 1998. The letter has been reprinted in my book of essays on public policy, *The Wind of the Hundred Days: How Washington Mismanaged Globalization* (Cambridge: MIT Press, 2001).

tellectual developments that often interacted with, and at times were even triggered by, the economic events and concerns of the time. In fact, it is remarkable that the cry of a "crisis" in free trade has been raised over the last two centuries by economists as diverse and renowned as John Maynard Keynes (who led the critics) and John Hicks (who lamented the crisis instead).

In each of these instances, which I shall proceed presently to review, the key element causing the crisis for free trade was the presence of a "market failure" or what, following my work and terminology introduced in the 1960s, is also characterized as the presence of a "distortion."

Heuristically, the argument is best seen as follows. The case for free trade rests on the extension to an open economy of the case for market-determined allocation of resources. If market prices reflect "true" or social costs, then clearly Adam Smith's invisible hand can be trusted to guide us to efficiency; and free trade can correspondingly be shown to be the optimal way to choose trade (and associated domestic production). But if markets do not work well, or are absent or incomplete, then the invisible hand may point in the wrong direction: free trade cannot then be asserted to be the best policy. Theoretically, this leads to the first of two key insights or propositions of the postwar theory of commercial policy.[10]

---

[10] This proposition owes, in my view, to Gottfried Haberler's article "Some Problems in the Pure Theory of International Trade," *Economic Journal* 60 (1950): 223–40, where he considered distortions such as sticky real wages and argued that free trade could worsen welfare. He did not

PROPOSITION 1

*In the presence of market failure (i.e., distortion), free
trade is not necessarily the best policy.*

One (in my view, unimportant) implication is that, since free
trade equilibrium in such a distorted economy is clearly suboptimal, an infinitesimal tariff would generally improve welfare, thus yielding a "second-best" argument for protection.

The other implication, of course, is that one can generate,
by postulating a yet different market failure, an endless number of cases where freeing trade from an arbitrarily given
level of protection is harmful rather than helpful, immiserizing rather than enriching.

This latter implication is, in fact, key to understanding the
occasional crises in the case for free trade that plagued the
profession over two centuries of economic thought and policy analysis.

---

draw the conclusion as sharply and as a generic problem for free trade
under distortions as I do above; but it certainly stimulated my own thinking in this direction when I read the paper as a student at Cambridge.

The other proposition, which is the key and most important insight of
the postwar theory of commercial policy in my view and that of most
other trade theorists as well, is that if another policy is deployed to offset
the market failure, the case for free trade gets restored. As I say below, in
the next section, this is obvious once you see it; but the fact is that for
over 150 years, no one really saw it that way and that the insight, when
developed first in "Domestic Distortions, Tariffs, and the Theory of Optimal Subsidy," the paper that I and V. K. Ramaswami published in the
Journal of Political Economy 71 (1963): 44–50, revolutionized the way we
have thought about free trade ever since.

Market Failures or Distortions from the 1840s

Let me now give you an eye-scan of the main such market-failure-centered crises or challenges to the doctrine of free trade.

But, in doing so, let me also clarify one central point that will otherwise escape economists not exposed to the modern theory of commercial policy. This is that, when we speak of free trade from the viewpoint of *national* advantage, distortion will characterize the economy even when there is no domestic market failure but the economy enjoys monopoly power *in trade* (i.e., its terms of trade depend on its volume of trade) even while its producers are atomistic and competitive.[11]

This is because the true social cost of unit imports is no longer measured by the average world prices that free trade transposes to your domestic producers for their allocation decisions; it is instead the marginal world prices. Under free trade, such a "large" country (i.e.. one that can influence its terms of trade) will then trade too much, and the case arises for an optimal tariff.

As it happens, this is the oldest case against free trade and goes back to Torrens in 1844;[12] and it played a role in the

---

[11] General nontrade theorists are used to thinking entirely in terms of Pareto-optimality of a competitive system, and this corresponds to talking about cosmopolitan advantage or worldwide efficiency in the theory of commercial policy. In *that* context, there is no distortion if a country has (unexercised) monopoly power. Distortions or market failures therefore cannot be defined except by reference to what your problem is.

[12] Cf. Robert Torrens, *The Budget: On Commercial and Colonial Policy* (London: Smith, Elder, 1848).

parliamentary debates at the time that Prime Minister Peel repealed England's Corn Laws to introduce (unilateral) free trade in England in 1848. As we shall see, the 1980s literature on trade policy under imperfect product markets has an affinity to this early example of free trade's suboptimality and hence inappropriateness relative to an optimal tariff because of what can be properly called a distortion or market failure in a country's "external" market(s).

The other classic exception to the case for free trade also relies on market failure. This is the case for an infant industry tariff that John Stuart Mill made in 1848 in one simple but elegant paragraph that is sufficiently carefully phrased to pass our scrutiny even today.[13] One can fit a number of possible failures in "domestic" producer or labor markets into this hat; though the ease with which infant industry protection has been invoked for protectionist purposes in reality has given some credence to the fearful prophecy of Corn Law League activist for free trade, Richard Cobden, that this one paragraph of Mill would do more damage than all the good done by his many writings on political economy![14]

We must jump three-quarters of a century to get the next important analytical challenge to free trade, but one that was more frontal and with yet more political salience. It came with the onset of the Great Depression. In his lecture on *Free Trade and Modern Economics* in 1951 to the Manchester

[13] Cf. John Stuart Mill, *Principles of Political Economy* (London: Longmans, Green, 1848).

[14] Cf. Quoted by Douglas Irwin, *Against the Tide: An Intellectual History of Free Trade* (Princeton: Princeton University Press, 1995), 128–29.

Statistical Society, John Hicks recounted how the unemployment of these years had seriously undermined the belief in free trade:[15]

> The main thing which caused so much liberal opinion in England to lose its faith in free trade was the helplessness of older liberalism in the face of massive unemployment, and the possibility of using import restriction as an element in an active programme fighting unemployment. One is, of course, obliged to associate this line of thought with the name of Keynes. It was this, almost alone, which led Keynes to abandon his early belief in Free Trade.

As it happens, Keynes's eventual breaking of ranks with free traders in Britain had been hinted at in 1930 in *A Treatise on Money* and also in his evidence before the Macmillan committee in February 1930, where he offered the view that tariffs, while unwise as a long-term policy, could immediately help fight the slump. This view became more pronounced through 1931, culminating in Keynes's celebrated controversy with Lionel Robbins and a riposte to Keynes's apostasy by Robbins, Hicks, and others in 1932 in *Tariffs: The Case Examined.*[16]

The Keynesian warming to protection in times of unemployment due to deficiency of aggregate demand evidently

[15] Cf. John R. Hicks, *Essays in World Economics* (Oxford: Clarendon Press, 1959), 48.

[16] Cf. J. M. Keynes, *A Treatise on Money* (London: Macmillan, 1931); and W. Beveridge, ed., *Tariffs: The Case Examined* (New York: Longmans, Green, 1932). See also the discussion of Keynes's views in Irwin, *Against*

derived from the notion that tariffs could divert aggregate demand from foreign to domestic goods. But from the viewpoint that I am setting forth here about the role of market failures in undermining the case for free trade, it is equally possible for us to see that since the social cost of labor in a situation of massive unemployment is clearly less than its (market) wage,[17] this is a market failure, and free trade is no longer a compelling policy. That the optimal policy mix would still be to remove that market failure by creating sufficiently more aggregate demand, instead of diverting a given aggregate demand towards yourself, and then holding on to free trade, is a matter that I shall turn to in the context of proposition 2 in the next section.

While the 1930s witnessed therefore the Keynesian defection from free trade, and its importance in providing intellectual support for the outbreak of competitive raising of trade barriers (and currency depreciations) should not be underestimated, these years also saw the emergence of a threat to free trade from an altogether different direction. It came, not from economic circumstance as had the Keynesian case for protection from the huge slump, but entirely from autonomous theoretical progress: and that too in a curiously tangential way.

As the 1920s ended, Edward Chamberlin in 1929 and Joan Robinson in 1931 independently came up with important

---

the Tide; and Barry Eichengreen, "Keynes and Protection," *Journal of Economic History* 44 (1984): 363–73.

[17] Keynesian unemployment is attributable to a sticky market wage such that it does not fall and increase hiring to the level of full employment.

theoretical analysis of imperfect competition, opening up to systematic exploration the middle ground between perfect competition and pure monopoly.[18] The result was to undermine the notion that market prices reflected social costs, calling into question more widely the virtue of laissez-faire and more narrowly the case for free trade. As Hicks observed in his 1951 lecture:[19]

> the Monopoly-Competition argument . . . is of much less practical importance than the others [e.g. the Keynesian one], but it deserves at least a passing mention, because of the undoubted influence which it undoubtedly exercises— in a negative sort of way—upon the minds of economics students. . . . If apparent costs only equal true costs under conditions of perfect competition and competition is hardly ever perfect, the bottom seems to drop out of the Free Trade argument. This is in fact a fair description of the state of mind which quite a number of economics students seem to have reached.

Two observations are in order for now. First, you will have noticed that what Hicks calls the "Monopoly-Competition argument" is little more and nothing less than the argument

---

[18] Cf. Edward Chamberlin, *The Theory of Monopolistic Competition* (Cambridge: Harvard University Press, 1929); and Joan Robinson, *The Economics of Imperfect Competition* (London: Macmillan, 1931).

[19] Hicks, *Essays in World Economics*, 46. He also remarks, "Free Trade is no longer accepted by economists, even as an ideal, in the way it used to be . . . the preponderance of economic opinion is no longer so certainly as it was on the Free Trade side" (41–42). Evidently, he is writing about English economists and economics students.

that imperfect competition in *product* markets can destroy the presumption that market prices will reflect social costs. But this is precisely the argument that emerged in the 1980s (a period I will address below) in the work of ⟨brilliant⟩ young trade theorists such as James Brander, Barbara Spencer, Paul Krugman, Elhanan Helpman, Avinash Dixit, Gene Grossman, and Jonathan Eaton. But whereas Hicks recorded how the reaction against free trade was essentially nihilistic because, as Hicks observed in the preface to *Value and Capital*, there was (despite the Chamberlin-Robinson revolution) no theoretically adequate way to deal with imperfect competition at the time, this was not so during the 1980s. In that latter period, the trade theorists could draw on the recent developments in the theory of industrial organization to fill out better the space between perfect competition and pure monopoly, so one could go beyond nihilism to say how precisely, if at all, free trade would have to be departed from under different types of imperfections (e.g., the small-group case of oligopoly versus the large-group case on which Chamberlin had made true progress).

Second, while Hicks (writing in 1951) was right to say that the argument had no political salience in the 1930s and later, this was not the case in the 1980s. The rise of Japan, the "diminished-giant syndrome" in the United States (hard to recollect now that the United States has emerged as what the French like to call a hyperpower),[20] the growth of compe-

---

[20] This term was introduced by me at the time and discussed especially in *Protectionism* (Cambridge: MIT Press, 1988). Some have called this syndrome *declinism*. See also my articles on the subject, reprinted in *A Stream of Windows: Unsettling Reflections on Trade, Immigration, and Democracy* (Cambridge: MIT Press, 1998).

tition among large firms producing differentiated products, and the conviction that Japan was not playing by rules of free trade, had all provided the necessary conditions for the monopoly-competition argument to have a public audience this time around!

The role of market failure or distortions in creating skepticism towards free trade within the economic profession took yet a different form after the Second World War. The newly independent developing countries were determined to use the "infant industry" argument of John Stuart Mill to push ahead with industrialization under an import substitution strategy.

Equally, they considered such industrialization to be essential for developing a modern society, expressing therefore what the theorists of commercial policy have come to call from the 1960s a "noneconomic objective." This would trigger a different kind of commercial-policy literature, one that asked what kinds of departures from free trade would *minimize* the cost of achieving such an objective.[21]

But this case for infant industry protection was strongly reinforced by the prevailing view that the developing countries were marked by a number of *factor* market imperfections (some of which were in fact cited as the underlying

[21] This literature has a heuristically "dual" relationship to the literature that I cite and use under the rubric of proposition 2 below, as noted in my article "Generalized Theory of Distortions and Welfare" in *Trade, Balance of Payments, and Growth: Essays in Honor of Charles P. Kindleberger,* ed. by Bhagwati, Ronald Jones, Robert Mundell, and Jaroslav Vanek (Amsterdam: North Holland, 1970).

reasons for infant industry protection of new manufactures). These distortions in the factor markets fell into three broad groups: a distorting wage differential between rural and urban sectors despite flexible wages; identical wages across sectors but a generalized sticky wage; and a sticky or minimum wage in one sector but flexible wages that could then endogenously lead to a wage differential between sectors.

In all these cases, it was clear that market prices would then diverge from social costs, thus raising new arguments for protection. In fact, in his 1958 article, Everett Hagen developed a case for protecting manufactures precisely because a distorting wage differential operated to raise inefficiently the cost of labor to manufacturers.[22] So did the argument of Gottfried Haberler that sticky wages could lead to real income loss from resulting unemployment under free trade that could outweigh the gains from trade.[23]

The final revolt against free trade from within would emerge in the 1980s, prompted (you may recall) by the in-

[22] This is the so-called Manoelesco argument for protection in developing countries. In fact, the Bhagwati-Ramaswami paper "Domestic Distortions," which led to proposition 2 below and revolutionized the theory of commercial policy, owed directly to the argument of the Hagen paper and of the 1950 Haberler paper, "Some Problems."

[23] Haberler, "Some Problems." The important theoretical papers by Richard Brecher on generalized sticky wages in an open economy are an outgrowth of the analysis initiated by Haberler. Cf. Richard Brecher, "Minimum Wage Rates and the Pure Theory of International Trade," *Quarterly Journal of Economics* 88, no. 1 (1974): 98–116; and "Optimum Commercial Policy for a Minimum Wage Economy," *Journal of International Economics* 4 (May 1974): 139–50.

tense competition felt by the United States from Japan and
the fear that the U.S. hegemony was yielding to a Pacific one.
Thus, while the 1980s shared with the 1950s through 1970s
the distinction of having the theory of free trade extended
into an analysis of the consequences of imperfect competition, there was one dramatic difference. Where the earlier
period had been concerned with *factor* market imperfections,
the latter period was concerned with *product* market imperfections. The former had fed protectionism in the developing
countries; the latter would do so in the developed countries.

From the viewpoint of the positive theory of international
trade, the "new" theory of imperfect competition that took
center stage was evidently a major conceptual advance. But
in the long view of the market failures that I have outlined
and particularly in the perspective of the 1930s challenge
from the monopoly-competition argument, the 1980s challenge to the theory of free trade was fairly conventional.

But in the public-policy arena, the 1980s challenge was
seen as novel because the implication of the "new" theory
for free trade was presented, not as an old insight that was
now refined (in terms of policy implications for the nature
of departure from free trade that was called for, these implications now drawn elegantly by exploiting the latest ad-
vances in the theory of industrial organization that were not
available earlier), but as a radical new insight into, and as a
powerful and unprecedented dent, in the case for free trade.

In fact, Paul Krugman, in his youthful surrender to irra-
tional exuberance, went so far as to propagate the view that,
in light of these new developments, it was not possible now
to oppose protectionism on theoretical grounds, that free
trade was passé, and that the case for it was now reduced to

one of empirical judgment.[24] Of course, this contention, which appeared like a confirmation of what protectionists had always suspected, had an electrifying effect on them; but, as is evident, it was not credible, as you will immediately appreciate if your mind has not been wandering during this lecture!

Besides, every economic policy has to reflect empirical judgment. That judgment relates essentially to deciding which theoretical model is applicable to the problem at hand (and then also choosing the correct parameters to feed into the selected model). Of the numerous market failures that I have touched upon, you would have to decide which are pertinent and which might be considered to be theoretical *curiosa*. Thus, the objection raised by Torrens to Peel's repeal of the Corn Laws on the ground that Britain had sufficient monopoly power in trade to require a positive optimal tariff was obviously a theoretical objection; but it was being applied to the British context of that time. Today, the weight of the evidence seems to have settled in favor of Peel's position, with Douglas Irwin having argued convincingly (against Donald McCloskey's view) that Britain possessed significantly less monopoly power than McCloskey had presumed.[25]

---

[24] Cf. Paul Krugman, "Is Free Trade Passé?" *Journal of Economic Perspectives* 1 (1987): 131–44. Also see my earlier critique in "Is Free Trade Passé after All?" chapter 1 in my *Political Economy and International Economics,* ed. Douglas Irwin (Cambridge: MIT Press, 1991).

[25] Cf. Donald McCloskey, "Magnanimous Albion: Free Trade and British National Income, 1841–1881," *Explorations in Economic History* 17 (1980): 303–20; and Douglas Irwin, "Welfare Effects of British Free Trade: Debate and Evidence from the 1840s," *Journal of Political Economy* 96

Immiserizing Growth

In conclusion of this line of over 150 years of detractions from the case for free trade since Adam Smith's time, starting from Torrens and Mill, all centering on market failures or distortions of one kind or another, let me suggest yet another way in which theorists can understand why a distortion in place will undermine the case for free trade.

This has to do with the theory of *immiserizing growth*. In 1958, I published in the *Review of Economic Studies* what fortuitously turned out to be an influential paper showing that growth in an open economy with monopoly power in trade could immiserize it.[26] The key was that the primary gain from growth could be more than offset by the induced loss from a deterioration in the terms of trade. I established also the conditions under which this could happen. The paper was politically salient because the developing countries, you will recall, were bent on an import substitution strategy and thought that my theoretical analysis gave them the underpinnings for their prescription.

In fact, it did. Because this paradox arose in a country practicing free trade when the postulated monopoly power in trade required instead an optimal tariff policy, the growth

---

(December 1988): 1142–64. The optimal tariff calculated by Irwin here is lower than what McCloskey had estimated; and Irwin also argues that the demonstration of British gains from freeing trade may have also reduced foreign tariffs, a general question that I take up in the last lecture.

[26] J. Bhagwati, "Immiserizing Growth: A Geometric Note," *Review of Economic Studies* 25 (1958): 201–5.

(through technical change or capital accumulation) was occurring in the presence of a distortion, that is, market failure. Presented with yet another case of immiserizing growth produced by Harry Johnson in the *Economic Journal* in 1967 where growth subject to a distorting tariff in a small country with no monopoly power led to immiseration,[27] I realized instantly, and wrote a sequel paper in the *Review of Economic Studies* in 1968, that the source of the paradox of immiserizing growth was the distortion.[28] The primary gain from growth, measured at optimal policies, was being overwhelmed by accentuated loss from the distortion. And to make my argument concrete, I produced added examples of immiserizing growth, using different distortions.

Why do I mention this? Because free trade is tantamount to augmenting your possibility set,[29] compared to autarky and restricted trade for a small country. If so, it is immediately obvious that you can get the kinds of examples of free trade's being inferior to autarky that Hagen and Haberler had produced: they were analytically identical to the para-

[27] H. G. Johnson, "The Possibility of Income Losses from Increased Efficiency or Factor Accumulation in the Presence of Tariffs," *Economic Journal* 77 (1967): 151–54.

[28] J. Bhagwati, "Distortions and Immiserizing Growth: A Generalization," *Review of Economic Studies* 35 (1968): 481–85.

[29] Just think of the free trade Baldwin locus. All this is spelled out, with many important applications and implications, in the chapter on immiserizing growth in the graduate textbook by Bhagwati, Arvind Panagariya, and T. N. Srinivasan, *Lectures on International Trade* (Cambridge: MIT Press, 1999), the second and enlarged edition of the Bhagwati and Srinivasan text.

doxes of immiserizing growth! Does this insight help? I daresay it does. For, there are usually different ways of looking
at a result; one appeals to some, another to others. As our
proverb goes: to each according to his taste. The Japanese
proverb puts it more pungently: some prefer nettles.

Returning to Free Trade: Fixing Domestic Distortions Directly

I must now recall the breakthrough that got us out of this
box into which distortions, or market failures, had landed
generations of economists espousing free trade. The solution
is so simple that it is hard to see its importance and why the
paper that I wrote (jointly with the late V. K. Ramaswami)
in 1963 in the *Journal of Political Economy* stating it has
turned out to influence all subsequent contributions to the
theory of commercial policy.[30]

Coming from both Haberler and Hagen, we saw in a flash
that free trade could not be declared the necessarily best
policy for a small country (or even a better policy than autarky for any country, small or large) in the presence of a
distortion. But we also realized, as no one had pointedly

---

[30] See, for instance, Arvind Panagariya, "Bhagwati and Ramaswami:
Why It *Is* a Classic," University of Maryland, 1999, typescript; Douglas
Irwin, "Profile: Jagdish Bhagwati," *Review of International Economics*,
1997; and contributions by T. N. Srinivasan and by Paul Krugman in *The
Political Economy of Trade: Essays in Honor of Jagdish Bhagwati*, ed. Robert
Feenstra, Gene Grossman, and Douglas Irwin (Cambridge: MIT Press,
1995).

done earlier, that if a suitable policy was addressed to offsetting that distortion, then we could get back to endorsing
free trade.

Of course, if the distortion was in domestic markets, that
meant that a domestic policy, suitably designed and targeted
to offsetting that distortion, could be combined with free
trade to produce the best outcome. If, however, the distortion or market failure occurred in external markets, then the
suitable policy to offset it would involve trade (tariff and
subsidy) policy, and free trade, ipso facto, could not be
maintained in the optimal equilibrium.

What the Bhagwati-Ramaswami analysis did, then, was to
eliminate the earlier, nihilistic loss of faith in free trade in
the presence of market failure. Arguing that free trade could
be maintained as the best policy when used in conjunction
with a domestic policy addressed to the domestic distortion,
the Bhagwati-Ramaswami analysis narrowed hugely the use
of protection to the case(s) where the distortion occurred in
the foreign or external markets.[31] So let me formulate the
second, more important proposition of the postwar theory
of commercial policy.

---

[31] I omit other important legacies of the Bhagwati-Ramaswami article,
such as the rank-ordering of different policies in the presence of distortions, which have now become the standard toolkit of all trade theorists.
An important follow-up was my 1970 article "Generalized Theory of Distortions and Welfare," where the vast theoretical literature on optimal and
second-best interventions under a variety of distortions that followed the
1963 Bhagwati-Ramaswami article was synthesized and a set of propositions in the generalized theory of distortions and welfare in an open economy was formulated. T. N. Srinivasan's important article in Feenstra,

PROPOSITION 2

(1) Where the distortion is domestic, a domestic (tax-cum-subsidy) policy targeting it will be appropriate, and free trade can then be restored as the suitable first-best trade policy; and (2) Where the distortion is external, free trade must be departed from as part of the suitable first-best trade policy addressed to that distortion.

Yet another way in which one can view proposition 2 insightfully is in terms of the theory of economic policy. This theory says that, generally speaking, you need as many instruments as you have targets. This is best explained to the public at large by invoking the ancient proverb, which is possibly to be found in every culture, "You cannot kill two birds with one stone." Generally, you need two stones to kill two birds unless you have inhuman strength, the birds happen to get on to one trajectory from your position, and providence grants you good luck. If you have a domestic distortion, this requires that it be addressed by a domestic policy; and maximizing the gains from trade requires free trade. Thus, in the Hagen-Manoelesco case of a distorting wage differential where Hagen had argued for protection, Bhagwati and Ramaswami showed that the first-best policy consisted of a wage tax–cum–subsidy plus free trade. If a producer-market distortion occurred through uncompensated production externality, the first-best policy would be a production tax–cum–subsidy plus free trade.

Grossman, and Irwin, *Political Economy of Trade*, does the same for the vast literature on the theory of commercial policy since the early 1970s.

Tackling External Distortions: Restoring Free Trade Differently

The case for free trade was thus released in a significant way from the stranglehold that market failure had put on it over two centuries! This was victory enough, but it was not a total victory.

For where the nation-state had monopoly power in trade (the Torrens argument) or the firms had it (as in the 1930s monopoly-competition argument and in the 1980s imperfect competition argument), the distortion was in the external markets, and then the use of trade tariffs (and subsidies) remained theoretically part of the appropriate first-best policy intervention. So how would one deal with that? In fact, this problem was endemic to the question raised by the presence of imperfect competition in product markets: this *necessarily* created a distortion in the external market.

The Bhagwati-Ramaswami revolution furnished no help in this class of distortions. What would one do to resurrect the policy of free trade in this case? The answer lay in precisely the reaction to the monopoly-competition argument of the 1930s. Two lines of response had been made to this argument: both at a more general level of the efficiency of market allocations and hence the Pareto-optimality of the competitive system rather than the specifics of free trade.

The *first* is what might be called the Chicago School response. If the naked eye perceived imperfect competition, Chicago asked whether that was a significant enough imperfection. Was there not "as if" competition if you only looked at the matter carefully, econometrically testing for the hypothesis that the industry was as if competitive? If, therefore, in current conceptualization, markets were contestable, the presumed monopoly power and imperfect competition were not matters to worry about for policymaking. So econometrics became the handmaiden to slaying the doubts raised by the casual empiricism of the naked eye.[32] In terms of American slang, where one asks where the beef is in the hamburger, the question is, where's the beef? As it happens, the younger trade theorists of imperfect competition in product markets, such as Avinash Dixit and Gene Grossman,[33] came back to the fold of free trade precisely on the ground that the gains to be had from pursuing a policy of optimal departures from free trade in selected industries characterized by imperfect competition were not large enough to justify intervention.[34]

[32] So, I have argued, in my obituary of Harry Johnson, reprinted in *A Stream of Windows*, that econometrics became important in Chicago in these years. By contrast, mathematical economics, which, at least in the hands of Arrow, Debreu, and others, seemed to probe existence, uniqueness, and stability of the competitive system and thus throw up roadblocks to Adam Smith's otherwise persuasive case, was not so popular.

[33] See, in particular, Avinash Dixit, "International Trade Policy for Oligopolistic Industries," *Economic Journal* 94 (1984): 1–16; Gene Grossman, "Strategic Export Promotion: A Critique," in *Strategic Trade Policy and the New International Economics*, ed. Paul Krugman (Cambridge: MIT Press, 1996); and David Richardson, "Empirical Research on Trade Liberalization with Imperfect Competition: A Survey," *OECD Economic Studies*, spring 1989, 7–50.

[34] There is also an interesting literature justifying the small-country assumption for developing countries econometrically. Cf. James Reidel,

The *second* route back to free trade is more associated with the public choice school than with Chicago: but it is no stranger to Chicago. This response concedes that there is beef here. But it contends that intervention to take advantage of it may, indeed (in the more fashionable stronger version) will, make matters worse. In short, the invisible hand may be frail, but the visible hand is crippled.

This response has been embraced by many, including Paul Krugman in his firm retreat back to free trade, but must be regarded as resting on a view of government that may not be shared naturally by everyone. True, when one sees how special interests capture trade (and often other economic) policy, it is easy to understand why those of us who prescribe interventions as if they will always be implemented by politicians who are our puppets doing our bidding in the national interest are making a heroic assumption.[35] On the other hand, one cannot deny that some degree of general interest does affect policy outcomes.[36] So one could well be some-

---

"The Demand for LDC Exports of Manufactures: Estimates from Hong Kong," *Economic Journal* 98 (1988): 138–48; and Arvind Panagariya, Shekhar Shah, and Deepak Mishra, "Demand Elasticities in International Trade: Are They Really Low?" *Journal of Development Economics* 64, no. 2 (2001): 313–42.

[35] I use the phrasing *puppet government* instead of the *benign government* to describe conventional, politics-free theory of government that is simply assumed to take the economist's advice. This comes from my 1990 essay, "The Theory of Political Economy, Economic Policy, and Foreign Investment," reprinted as chapter 9 in my *Political Economy and International Economics*.

[36] See my more extended discussion of these issues in "Is Free Trade Passé?"

what agnostic on the probability of improving matters through intervention when there *is* beef.

But there is a good alternative argument that things could most likely get worse through trade intervention when there is imperfect competition in external markets: and that proceeds from the possibility of trade retaliation. For the traditional, Torrens variety of optimal tariff in the case of national monopoly power in trade, with firms competitive, it was generally believed, and Tibor Scitovsky underlined, that retaliation would make everyone worse off, and hence it was best to stick to free trade. But then, in a classic paper using the Cournot model of optimum tariff retaliation, Harry Johnson showed that the end result of a tariff war could be to leave the one that first used the optimum tariff still better off than under free trade. And Carlos Rodriguez restored the general presumption in favor of free trade by using optimum trade quotas rather than tariffs: an assumption that is more realistic for the 1930s after the infamous Smoot-Hawley tariff of the United States and the competitive raising of trade barriers worldwide.[37] Evidently, depending on what assumptions you make, it is possible to rescue the possibility that, despite retaliation, the initial use of an optimal tariff by a country with monopoly power in trade will leave it still better off than under free trade. But that reality is not certain,

[37] Cf. Tibor Scitovsky, "A Reconsideration of the Theory of Tariffs," *Review of Economic Studies* 9 (1942): 89–110; Harry Johnson, "Optimum Tariffs and Retaliation," *Review of Economic Studies* 21 (1953–54): 142–53; and Carlos Rodriguez, "The Non-equivalence of Tariffs and Quotas under Retaliation," *Journal of International Economics* 4 (1974): 295–98.

whereas it is surely overwhelmingly likely that even the small "little-beef" gains to be had from the use of trade barriers in the presence of external distortion will shrink further when retaliation takes place.

Theory of Directly Unproductive Profit-Seeking Activities: Reinforcing the Case for Free Trade

Thus, between (1) the theory of domestic distortions and welfare, whose central insights I have shown above to have revolutionized the case for free trade—contrary to those believers who think that little has changed since Adam Smith—and rescued it effectively from the historically countless domestic-distortions-defined detractions, and (2) the theoretical and econometric arguments that have deflated the plausibility of welfare-enhancing protectionist departure from free trade in the presence of varying forms of external monopoly power, we ended the twentieth century with a far firmer case for free trade than the one we inherited at the end of the Second World War.

But at least one more theoretical development of considerable importance has also strengthened that case greatly. It comes from an indirect route. Let me explain. Ever since the Harberger-Johnson estimates of the cost of protection, measured as the deadweight losses (the so-called Harberger triangles) that typically ran at 2–3 percent of GNP, there has been a sense that, even if free trade is the best policy, protection is not anything you need to worry about too much since the cost of it is rather small.

In my 1967 Frank Graham Lecture at Princeton, I rejected such a presumption by arguing several points.[38] First, even 2–3 percent of GNP was not small, and most economic reforms involved similar, or even smaller, shares of GNP. Next, it was important to remember that reforms were usually packaged together and a policy package of small-yielding reforms often added up to a large-yielding policy reform. Besides, dividing the gains from free trade by GNP always made the number look small. Then again, the Harberger-Johnson numbers inevitably depended on parametric assumptions about elasticities within postulated models, but it was easy to encounter realistic models where, as in the developing countries with heavy exchange and trade controls that I was talking about, it was possible to think realistically of larger losses from these protectionist policies. For instance, the lack of accessibility to imported components to repair a machine could hold up output, yielding in that case a huge loss equivalent to that of the entire plant, a situation in which the elasticities would be very different from those postulated in the Harberger-Johnson estimates.[39]

[38] Cf. "The Theory of Commercial Policy: Departures from Unified Exchange Rates," Special Papers in International Economics, No. 8, Princeton University, 1968; reprinted as chapter 1 in my collected essays, *International Economic Theory*, vol. 1, ed. Robert Feenstra (Cambridge: MIT Press, 1983).

[39] These and other ways in which protection could be harmful in a big way were brought home to me from the work that I did in the 1960s with Padma Desai for our book, under a large OECD project on trade and industrialization policies of several semi-industrialized developing coun-

What has happened since I wrote almost four decades ago, objecting to the inevitability of the smallness of the cost of protection and hence the possibility of indifference to trade reforms to bring about free trade, is that trade economists have moved steadily in favor of the view that the Harberger-Johnson estimates need to be revised upwards.[40]

Some of this has had to do with emphasis on freer trade's favorable effects *via* one or more factors such as (1) increased exploitation of economies of scale, (2) enhanced diversity of choice among differentiated goods, (3) what Harvey Leibenstein used to call x-efficiency (i.e., the effect of competition through openness on pressuring firms to upgrade the productivity of their resource use instead of "goofing off"), (4) the demonstrated possibility that trade can be a conduit for know-how that can (as with a public good) be appropriated without acquisition cost, and (5) increased marginal

---

tries, directed by Ian Little, Tibor Scitovsky, and Maurice Scott. Cf. Bhagwati and Desai, *India: Planning for Industrialization.*

[40] See, for instance, the recent articles by Robert Feenstra, "How Costly Is Protectionism?" *Journal of Economic Perspectives* 6 (1992): 159–78, and by Paul Romer, "New Goods, Old Theory, and the Welfare Costs of Trade Restrictions," *Journal of Development Economics* 43 (1994): 5–38, both arguing that the cost of protection is fairly large. Recall also from the text that in countries with import or exchange restrictions, there will be large costs arising from such forms of protectionism because they lead to inflexibilities: a screw may become difficult to import and an entire machine on an assembly line may go out! This idea has recently been formally modeled by Michael Kremer, "The O-Ring Theory of Economic Development," *Quarterly Journal of Economics* 108, no. 3 (1993): 551–75.

efficiency of capital, leading to enhanced productive investment thanks to integration into world markets.[41]

But an important cause of this revisionism in favor of a large cost of protection has lain in the domain of political-economy theory that I have christened the theory of *directly unproductive profit-seeking* (DUP) activities.

Following Anne Krueger's important 1974 *American Economic Review* paper on the rent-seeking society, which basically argued that quotas fetched rents and then led to rent-seeking activity that compounded the cost of protection by leading to wasteful use of resources in chasing rents instead of producing goods and services that would add to national income, I introduced the DUP concept in my own 1980 *Journal of Political Economy* paper, which was both more general and free from some central problems inherent in the rent-seeking conceptualization.

The essence of the argument was that resources were being diverted to earn income in ways that did not produce goods and services. So it was not helpful to confine it to seeking that was triggered by quantitative-restrictions-generated rents. It could be extended readily, and needed to be, to phenomena such as smuggling to make an income by bypassing the legal channels of taxed trade, or to chasing revenues produced by price rather than quantity restrictions (e.g., to tariff-revenue-seeking as well).

---

[41] This argument has been developed by me, in the context of explaining the East Asian miracle, in "The Miracle That Did Happen: Understanding East Asia in Comparative Perspective," reprinted as chapter 4 in *The Wind of the Hundred Days.*

Besides, one had to distinguish between direct and indirect welfare effects. If a distorting tariff or a quota was in place, then the act of seeking them and the waste of resources used in chasing them was directly or at source harmful, but, because of the distorted suboptimal situation in which it was arising, it could lead indirectly or eventually to a gain of welfare. In other words, adding one distortion to another does not necessarily add to welfare loss, but may subtract from it. Thus, the unproductive profit-seeking activity in question could not be assumed, as proponents of rent-seeking were wont to do, to be necessarily wasteful in its final outcome as against its immediate impact.

Hence, I moved away from the notion of rents (with its connotation of quota-generated windfall profits) as too restrictive and felt that the concept and phrasing should simply refer to unproductive profit-seeking (which could be activities other than chasing rents). I also felt that the concept must explicitly recognize the fact that the waste in question was direct, as indirectly it may add to welfare if it was integrally triggered by policies such as trade barriers that had resulted in a highly distorted economy. The result was the concept and phrase of directly unproductive profit-seeking activities.[42]

---

[42] I have a series of theoretical papers on these and related issues, among them "Directly-Unproductive Profit-Seeking (DUP) Activities," *Journal of Political Economy* 90 (1982): 988–1002; "DUP Activities and Rent Seeking," *Kyklos* 36 (1983): 634–37; and *The New Palgrave* entry "Directly Unproductive Profit-Seeking (DUP) Activities," reprinted along with my other essays on DUP activities in *Political Economy and International Eco-*

Whether you wish to stick to the narrower concept of rent-seeking or to the broader concept of DUP activities, the fact is that the cost of protection *can* be higher with it than when you measure it Harberger-Johnson style as the deadweight loss from the departure from free trade. Indeed, I believe that this is likely to be so except in very highly distorted economies where resources have a negative shadow price at the margin.[43]

We go, then, to measuring the cost of protection, not just as the deadweight loss from it, but also adding to it the loss from the DUP activities associated with it.

But once we think of DUP activities, we need to distinguish sharply between two main types that have conceptually very different implications for arguments about the added cost of protection:

- *Upstream* DUP activities, which relate to the endogenizing of the tariff or trade quota and hence essen-

nomics. In some of the important papers on the subject, I have also collaborated with T. N. Srinivasan and with Richard Brecher: e.g. Bhagwati and Srinivasan, "Revenue-Seeking: A Generalization of the Theory of Tariffs," *Journal of Political Economy* 88 (1980): 1069–87; and Bhagwati, Brecher, and Srinivasan, "DUP Activities and Economic Theory," reprinted as chapter 7 in *Political Economy and International Economics.*

[43] There *are* instances of such economies, of course. T. N. Srinivasan, Henry Wan Jr., myself, Michael Mussa, and others have written extensively on this subject. Its mirror-image relationship to the phenomenon of immiserizing growth, discussed earlier, has also been extensively remarked upon. See in particular chapter 38 in Bhagwati, Panagariya, and Srinivasan, *Lectures on International Trade.*

tially to the cost of lobbying (or what might be called in the rent-seeking terminology "rent-creating" activity).

• *Downstream* DUP activities (the focus of Krueger's analysis), which relate instead to seeking activities triggered by the given tariff or quota: for example, in the case of tariff revenue, these revenues may be sought by lobbies that expend resources to do so, just as trade quotas are sought by lobbies because of the premiums they fetch.[44]

The upstream DUP activities raise a fundamental conceptual problem: how can the lobbying costs, even when measured properly as positive,[45] be attributed to protection meaningfully when the political process is endogenized to solve for the observed level of protection whose total cost we seek to measure?[46] To argue that the lobbying costs must be added to the conventional cost of observed but politically determined protection is to effectively say: Imagine a politics-free world where the politically determined tariff is imposed without the politics, calculate its cost conventionally (à la Harberger-Johnson), then add the lobbying costs

---

[44] Induced smuggling, when using resources as it almost always does, would be another instance.

[45] On this question, see my clarifications in "Lobbying and Welfare," *Journal of Public Economics* 14 (1980): 355–63; and "Lobbying, DUP Activities, and Welfare: A Response to Tullock," *Journal of Public Economics* 19 (1982): 335–41.

[46] This question has been extensively addressed in Bhagwati, Brecher, and Srinivasan, "DUP Activities."

implied by the loss of resources expended on the political
lobbying that has led to the tariff being what it is. But that
lobbying cost is really the cost of the *political process*, and
not the cost of the observed protection in any meaningful
sense that I can think of![47]

But there is no such conceptual problem with the downstream DUP activities. They will add to the conventional
Harberger-Johnson cost of protection (ruling out as im-
probable in most cases the possibility of the paradox of beneficial DUP activity as discussed above). Whether they are
large—Anne Krueger's estimate of their cost for Turkey,
looking at the entire Turkish set of licensing restrictions, was
of the order of 40 percent of GNP—or small depends on
your view of how a specific economic-cum-political regime
works. If everyone expects, for example, the rulers' brothers-
in-law to get the revenues or the rents, then few will waste
resources trying to get them (though, I daresay, some resources will be devoted by a handful of optimistic aspirants
to becoming a brother-in-law).[48] And indeed there is now a

---

[47] One can only say that if somehow the politics of making and oppos-
ing tariffs were eliminated by a constitutional amendment mandating free
trade, then we would know (for the specific politics built into one's political-economy model) what gains we would have in terms of freed up resources plus the avoided conventional cost of protection. This is true, at
best, only for protectorates or colonies.

[48] See, in particular, the important paper by Arye Hillman and John
Riley, "Politically Contestable Rents and Transfers," *Economics and Politics*
1 (1989): 17–39.

literature on the subject, getting away from Krueger's "competitive" assumption that a dollar worth of rents will lead to a dollar worth of resource waste. It is likely, in my judgment, that many systems will indeed show a downstream DUP cost that would more than double the deadweight losses of the Harberger-Johnson variety.

Free Trade and Growth

So the case for free trade today has surmounted, in my view, the difficulties that have afflicted it for over a century and a half. But while there is always a tendency to carry one's success too far, I must say that the recent debate over whether free trade (or rather freer trade) will lead to greater *growth* (and not just current welfare) goes also in the direction of adding to the virtues of free trade.

Of course, anyone who knows theory well also knows immediately that the case for free trade, while valid in an intertemporal setting (as argued cogently by Avinash Dixit), does not imply that a country will have a higher growth rate as well. Indeed, in a large variety of models free trade may actually reduce the growth rate or, in steady state, leave it unaffected.

Thus, consider the case where fiscal policy is not an available instrument to set the savings ratio at a desired level but is a function solely of market-determined income distribution. Imagine then a Harrod-Domar growth model where the growth rate depends on two variables: the (average) saving ratio divided by the (marginal) capital-output ratio. Free trade will minimize the latter but may reduce the former, thus lowering the growth rate on balance.[49]

On the other hand, in Robert Solow's neoclassical model of growth of the 1960s, trade policy *cannot* affect, in steady state, the growth rate. But then, as T. N. Srinivasan has emphasized, using the Feldman-Mahalanobis putty-clay model and the Cass-Koopmans model of optimal growth, there are models in which the steady state is not an exogenous constant and therefore they can be used to generate growth effects from choice of trade policy.[50]

So those who assert that free trade will also lead necessarily to greater growth *either* are ignorant of the finer nuances of theory and the vast literature to the contrary on the subject at hand *or* are nonetheless basing their argument on a different premise: that is, that the preponderant evidence on the issue (in the postwar period) suggests that freer trade tends to lead to greater growth after all. In fact, where theory includes several models that can lead in different directions, the policy economist is challenged to choose the model that is most appropriate to the reality she confronts. And I would

[49] See, for instance, the careful analysis by Prasanta Pattanaik, "Trade, Distribution, and Saving," *Journal of International Economics* 4 (1974): 77–82, which formally relates the rate of saving in the conventional two-by-two model to trade policy via income-distributional impact of the trade policy.

[50] See, in particular, T. N. Srinivasan, "Trade Orientation, Trade Liberalization, and Economic Growth," in *Development, Duality, and the International Economic Regime: Essays in Honor of Gustav Ranis,* ed. Gary Saxonhouse and T. N. Srinivasan (Ann Arbor: Michigan University Press, 1999).

argue that, in the present instance, we must choose the approaches that generate favorable outcomes for growth when trade is liberalized.

That, in fact, is the substance of the response by Srinivasan and me to Dani Rodrik's recent critique of us and others (chiefly Bela Balassa, Anne Krueger, and, most recently, Jeffrey Sachs) who have argued for this relationship.[51]

But then one may grow more ambitious and look for yet other good things in life that might follow from free trade. For instance, does free trade also promote democracy? One could argue this proposition by a syllogism: openness to the benefits of trade brings prosperity that, in turn, creates or expands the middle class that then seeks the end of authoritarianism.[52] This would fit well with the experience in South

[51] Since the issues need careful argumentation, it is best to read them directly and at necessary length in Srinivasan and Bhagwati, "Outward-Orientation and Development: Are Revisionists Right?" chapter 1 in *Trade, Development, and Political Economy: Essays in Honour of Anne O. Krueger,* ed. Deepak Lal and Richard Snape (London: Palgrave, 2001). The paper is also on our websites. See also Francisco Rodriguez and Dani Rodrik, "Trade Policy and Economic Growth: A Skeptic's Guide to Cross-National Evidence," NBER Working Paper No.W7081, 1999. Its critique of the Sachs-Warner regression findings is well taken; but we discount both Sachs-Warner and Rodriguez-Rodrik types of cross-country regressions as inappropriate to a meaningful analysis of the complex questions involved. See Jeffrey Sachs and Aaron Warner, "Economic Reforms and the Process of Global Integration," *Brookings Papers on Economic Activity* 1995:1–118.

[52] Edward Mansfield, Helen Milner, and Peter Rosendorff, "Free to Trade: Democracies, Autocracies, and International Trade," *American Po-*

Korea, for instance. It was also the argument that changed a lot of minds when the issue of China's entry into the WTO came up in the U.S. Congress recently. I guess there is something to it.

But then one must also contend with the many today who argue *against* free trade on such grounds. They contend that free trade is incompatible with important broader goals such as egalitarian income distribution, environmental protection, labor standards, and human rights. Thus, even as the doctrine of free trade has emerged triumphant over the conventional challenges that I dealt with in this lecture, it now faces a new and original crisis. I turn to it in my next lecture.

---

litical Science Review 94 (2000): 305–21, have interestingly argued for the reverse relationship: that is, that pairs of democracies tend to reduce trade barriers more than mixed-country pairs.

LECTURE 2

"Fair Trade," Income Distribution, and Social Agendas: Using Trade Theory to Meet New Challenges

A Medley of Charges

The Folly of "Fair Trade": The American Virus

Unequal Environmental and Labor Standards
as Unfair Trade

Does Free Trade Damage the Environment?

Advancing Social and Moral Agendas: Free Trade
and Appropriate Governance

Other Applications of the Principle of
Two Birds and Two Stones

The Fear of the Trade Unions: Threat to Real Wages

Free Trade and Poverty in Poor Countries

THE crisis in which free trade finds itself today is different from the ones that occurred from the 1930s to the 1980s and were sketched in the first lecture. All of the latter essentially had to do with the contention that free trade would not maximize the size of the pie we could make from our resources, know-how, and trading possibilities.

Today, however, the issue is *not* whether free trade or protection is more effective in that regard. We have, if I am right in what I argued in lecture 1, settled *that* issue. The questions now are quite different (though, of course, in some instances there are historical precedents, but not for the intensity with which they occupy public space today).

In an essential way, the current issues are more potent and potentially lethal to free trade. The historical challenges were generally a result of occasional cerebral differences that prompted serious economists to defect from time to time from the cause of free trade. When these doubts intersected with economic circumstance (such as the Great Depression and its aftermath in the 1930s or the Japanese competitive success in the 1980s), the political salience of these dissensions was considerable since free trade's opponents could cite the heretics to their advantage.

But the perennial and persistent public-policy fights for free trade, in the end, were with protectionists who cared little about the size of the pie and more about their own slice of it. In short, the free traders could, when their doubts were resolved, claim that they were looking at the "general inter-est," while the run-of-the-mill and mainstream protection-ists typified the "special interests."

Hence we had attempts in the theory of political economy, as by the late Mancur Olson who first advanced the free-rider argument, to explain why concentrated and easy-to-mobilize producer interests, which typically signified specific interests geared to protecting their industries from interna-tional competition, tended to overwhelm the diffuse and dif-ficult-to-organize consumer interests that translated into the general interest.[1]

The proponents of free trade therefore started from, or at least could always claim, the higher moral ground. But to-day's challengers of free trade often fight our general interest with theirs; and the most vociferous among them even claim the higher moral ground. And since our case is more taxing on the mind and theirs is plainer to the view, the public-policy debate has put the proponents of free trade into a battle that is harder than ever to wage.

A Medley of Charges

The detractors of free trade today are many, and their com-plaints range over several issues. Indeed, some of them fire off their cannons in all directions. Thus, at a Cambridge Union debate with the leading English environmentalist Teddy Goldsmith, an ardent opponent of free trade, almost

---

[1] Cf. Mancur Olson, *The Logic of Collective Action* (Cambridge: Harvard University Press, 1965).

of any trade I thought, I found myself facing an impassioned but illogical opponent who sincerely believed, without systematic evidence, that trade was responsible for damage to the environment, for the sorry state of women, indeed for many evils that I had lacked the imagination to lay at the door of free trade. So, being in England, where wit wins you an argument, I replied by recalling the 1831 novella of Balzac, *The Wild Ass's Skin* (*La peau de chagrin* in French). The central character, Raphael, has a terrible condition: when he desires a beautiful woman, the talisman in shape of the ass's skin that he has been tempted into accepting shrinks and, with it, his life span as well. So, to go to the opera where he cannot avoid seeing lovely women around him, Raphael carries a special "monocle whose microscopic lens, skillfully inserted, destroy[s] the harmony of the loveliest features and [gives] them a hideous aspect." Looking through this monocle, Raphael sees only ugly women and is able to enjoy unscathed the glorious music that he loves. Mr. Goldsmith, I added, you seem to have with you a similar monocle, except that when you use it and see us wonderful free traders, you find us turned into ugly monsters. Our angel's halo turns into the devil's horns!

So where do I draw the line for this lecture? If I do not draw any, I can drown both you and me in a sea of superficially persuasive complaints and my responses to them. Instead I will focus on a few major areas that help me bring many (though not all) of these complaints on board, while also providing an analytically helpful way of systematizing them.

In essence, the new critiques divide into

• Demands for "fair trade" that either mask protectionism or degenerate into it, in both cases charging that free trade lacks fairness and that fair trade restores it
• Concerns that free trade harms the environment
• Charges that free trade (and its chief institution, the WTO) is incompatible with the advancement of social and moral agendas
• Fears that free trade hurts the real wages of workers and that rich countries trading with poor countries create poor in the rich countries; and, in poor countries, that free trade accentuates poverty

You can see right away, from this list, that the proponents of free trade confront opponents who claim fairness, social justice, nature, and moral purpose on their side. But I hope to show that not all, possibly nothing, is lost. And, in so doing, I again hope to show how the insights from the postwar theory of commercial policy and from other developments in the theory of trade and welfare can be valuable assets to us.

The Folly of "Fair Trade": The American Virus

The notion that when your trading partners have less open markets than your country does, this implies unfair trade and justifies protection, has been around for a long time. In response economists have usually argued that it is absurd to deny ourselves the benefits of free trade simply because of what others do in their trade policy. Remember that Joan

Robinson used to say, if others throw rocks into their harbor, that is no reason to throw rocks into our own.[2]

But the American policymakers have now gone well beyond the question of unfairness, in the sense of asymmetry in *trade* openness. They have been elevating asymmetries in *domestic* policies and institutions to a definition of unfair trade. Indeed, they have, through their infamous Section 301 legislation in the Omnibus Trade and Competitiveness Act of 1998, even sought to impose their consequent demands for harmonization on foreign nations and their firms by threats of trade retaliation. Thus, Section 301 gave to the executive the authority, even lay down the duty, to condemn other nations (under a so-called Super 301 provision) as unfair traders and then to follow up with tariff retaliation simply because they indulged in what America had unilaterally decided were unreasonable practices. I have called this *aggressive unilateralism* and will say more on it in the next lecture.[3] It is a practice that has been condemned worldwide; and today the use of Section 301 in this unilateral and discriminatory fashion outside of an existing trade obligation has been practically declared WTO-illegal.

I can identify four reasons for this insidious development in the United States, where the arguments on unfair trade

[2] In the last lecture, I return to this question of unilateral trade liberalization in greater depth.

[3] See my 1990 Harry Johnson Lecture, published as *The World Trading System at Risk* (Princeton: Princeton University Press, 1991); and Bhagwati and Hugh Patrick, eds., *Aggressive Unilateralism* (Ann Arbor: University of Michigan Press, 1991).

have intruded heavily into the political space, aiding the cause of protectionism—since virtually any asymmetry with another country can be cited as tantamount to unfair trade.

First, fairness rather than justice is the defining moral principle in the United States, as compared to the more socially structured European and Japanese societies. So equality of access trumps equality of success; equal opportunity trounces equal outcomes. American protectionists, compared to those elsewhere, have therefore found it strategically smarter to use "unfair trade" as their political weapon against foreign firms even as it has become unfashionable and unproductive—thanks, in no small measure, to our success in strengthening the case for free trade and because of the dramatic postwar success of open societies and economies and the contrasting failure of the autarkic ones—to seek protection by claiming that you cannot compete.

Second, intensification of competition worldwide and the "thinning" of comparative advantage have meant that firms increasingly look over their rivals' shoulders, objecting to all sorts of advantages that these rivals allegedly enjoy from differential domestic policies and institutions. They ask typically for level playing fields, by which they mean the equalization of burdens, the harmonization of costs, through the ironing out of as many differences as possible across countries.[4]

Third, the American sense of decline in the 1980s and early 1990s, or what in the first lecture I called the *diminished-giant syndrome*, also fueled the steady drift to fair

[4] See the opening chapter, "A New Epoch?" in *A Stream of Windows*.

trade, especially under President Clinton. True, he inherited this drift, but he accentuated it greatly. Thus, President Bush had largely refused to surrender to Japan-baiting as Japan rose to be a hugely successful rival. The talk grew of the twenty-first century as Asian, just as the nineteenth century was British and the twentieth century American. President Clinton came to the White House literally surrounded by Japanophobes who cried foul at every opportunity.[5] Japan was regarded as Superman and his evil foe Lex Luthor rolled into a fearsome juggernaut. Demonized thus, Japan was energetically pursued through President Clinton's first term as a wicked and unfair trader whose exports were predatory and imports were exclusionary.

Fourth, President Clinton's second term was witness to further capture by the fair traders from yet another angle. This time, the reinforcement came through regionalism (i.e., preferential trade agreements, or PTAs, a subject that I will address more fully in the last lecture). During the NAFTA debate, it was now Mexico's turn to be demonized as an unfair trader. Congressional Democratic leaders worked the political circuit thoroughly, to almost defeat NAFTA by claiming that free trade with Mexico was unfair because its

[5] I have little doubt that some of the economists who were more sensible had to go along to get along. Part of the reason was that the Clinton administration had come in, plagued by ceaseless and tasteless attacks on the president's sexual proclivities, barely surviving the so-called "bimbo" outbreaks. So I suspect that loyalty became a far more important trait in this administration than in others; and joining the Japan-obsessed crowd in the White House and in the administration became essential for survival.

labor and environmental standards were not as good as America's and because its democracy was flawed. Funnily, of course, at the time of the Canada–United States Free Trade Agreement, the boot was on the other foot: it was the Canadian opponents of the agreement who had objected to America's lower social standards! But the U.S. Congress was not gripped with self-examination and in a mood to reject CUFTA because of a disparity on standards running the wrong way. Evidently, "fair trade" is a handy tool, to be used to advantage against others, but not to be allowed to embarrass oneself.

An important lesson about PTAs emerges from this experience. When it comes to trade liberalization with only one or a few nations, in a typical PTA such as NAFTA, it is easy for protectionists to zero in on these few countries' warts and turn them into unfair trade issues. This is far more difficult to do when, as in the Uruguay Round, many countries negotiate several matters. Thus, Mexico's environmental, labor, and democratic shortcomings became defining issues during NAFTA; but the Uruguay Round debate was unscathed by them. Now, of course, such matters have grown into larger fair trade issues, like a laboratory-grown monster, and threaten the multilateral negotiations as well. But PTAs, or regional discriminatory trade agreements, were the Dr. Frankenstein.[6]

The rot that has set in by way of protectionists' ready resort to allegations of unfair trade is evident from the Clinton ad-

[6] I have been arguing this as a black mark against NAFTA, and against PTAs in general, for a long time. It is a point that is now increasingly conceded by observers of the trade policy scene in the United States.

ministration's response to the recent demands for steel protection. American spokespersons for trade, such as U.S. Trade
Representative Charlene Barshefsky and Commerce secretary
Richard Daly, have ceaselessly complained that America's
trade deficit was proof that inappropriate macroeconomic
policies by the European Union and Japan had led to inadequate growth and hence absorption of steel, so that they were
as good as unfair traders who must be held accountable for
an unmanageable growth in America's steel imports.

This is as ridiculous as it is symptomatic of the degenera-
tion of U.S. trade policy into a litany of unfair trade allegations. If the European Union and Japan were in fact using
protection to contain their imports and divert them on to
the United States, that would indeed be something to com-
plain about (from the viewpoint of steel producers, though
cheaper steel imports are good for the U.S. consumers and
producers who use steel). But the United States was saying
instead, "Your macroeconomic policies are not good
enough, and that is what makes you an unfair trader."
Would the U.S. policymakers have been happy if the EU and
Japan had accused them similarly of unfair trade in the
1980s when it was the Americans who were guilty of in-
competence at macroeconomic management? Of course,
this reversion to the rhetoric of unfair trade, flying in the
face of economic logic, made the politics of both demanding
and supplying protection to the ailing steel industry a lot
easier.

And so in the United States far too many politicians today
have turned into an unfair-trade-obsessed, cynically manip-
ulative lot. Broadly, with a few shining exceptions—such as
the former senator Daniel Patrick Moynihan among the

Democrats and Senator Phil Gramm, a former professor of economics, among the Republicans—they divide into two groups: the less disagreeable ones whose slogan is "free *and* fair trade," and the more disagreeable ones who insist on "fair trade *before* free trade." I might cite also the former president, who not merely fed the fair trade mania over Japan, but also called, in his State of the Union address in January 2000, for "a freer and fairer trading system for twenty-first century America."

The plain consequence is that the ceaseless refrain in favor of free trade by American politicians has nurtured an electorate that thinks of the United States as a fair trader and others, in varying degrees, as unfair traders.[7] The effect of this public perception, in turn, has been to encourage the thought in the country that free trade is both economically unwise and politically naive. And so, to the litany of hostile sentiments that come at free trade for reasons I sketched in the first lecture, I must add this unfortunate legacy of sloppy surrender by politicians to the rhetoric of fair trade.

[7] This tendency is perhaps endemic to the United States anyway. Thus, in a Washington debate with Senator Carl Levin of Detroit when Japan-bashing was at its peak and the senator was claiming that Japan's car market was closed while the American was open, I noted that the facts were quite the opposite to his claim: the United States had used voluntary export restraints against Japan, while Japan had not, so that one could argue that Japan's market was difficult to penetrate, not that it was closed, while the American market was "closed" but easy to penetrate. But, I added, I could understand why he still believed in America's comparative virtue: after all, I had come from one self-righteous country, India, to another, the United States!

Unequal Environmental and Labor Standards as Unfair Trade

A surrender to this dangerous rhetoric is particularly evident when one turns to the fair trade arguments that relate to differences in (domestic-pollution-related)[8] environmental and labor standards across countries. It has thus become routine to charge unfair trade when firms in foreign countries have lower environmental and labor standards because *(a)* they are then regarded as indulging in "social dumping" that needs to be countervailed by a tariff; and *(b)* it is feared that such differences in standards will trigger a "race to the bottom" that will undermine one's own higher standards. Demands for fair trade are then made on these foreign nations, asking them to raise their standards towards ours. Neither argument, however, is compelling.

Legitimacy of Diversity of Tax Burdens for Purely Domestic Pollution

Differences in standards typically reflect differences in fundamentals: in your initial conditions, your endowments and preferences. Thus, even when you have an identical desire to prevent domestic pollution per se, and you accept the princi-

---

[8] This section deals only with domestic, as distinct from transborder, pollution. It also does not extend to worrying about standards on altruistic grounds, an issue that is taken up below. For these distinctions, see my paper on linkages (between trade and environment and labor issues), reprinted in my collection of essays *The Wind of the Hundred Days*.

ple that polluters must pay, the pollution tax rates for identical carcinogens dumped into the local waters or the air can
be fully expected to differ across countries. Thus, if Mexico
has cleaner air and worse water than the United States
(where there are far more cars and also many water purifiers
and much bottled water), it is only to be expected that, given
the same willingness to address environmental issues, Mexico will tax water pollution more and air pollution less than
does the United States. You cannot then expect such legitimate tax burden differences to be countervailed as "social
dumping"! Diversity of tax burdens is thus fully legitimate.
To call it unfair competition is to betray ignorance of ele-
mentary economics.[9] But that is exactly what several American politicians have called for, including Democratic leadership all the way to former vice president Gore.

Empirical Irrelevance of Race to the Bottom

By contrast, the race-to-the-bottom argument is theoretically valid; where it fails is in its empirical relevance, in my
view. An uncoordinated Nash-equilibrium could well produce, under second-best conditions, outcomes where each
or a subset of countries will underachieve either or both
economic welfare and environmental goals compared to

[9] This argument has been spelled out more fully in the two volumes
published, from a substantial research project on the subject of harmonization and fair trade, in Bhagwati and Robert Hudec, eds., *Fair Trade and
Harmonization: Prerequisites for Free Trade?* 2 vols. (Cambridge: MIT
Press, 1996).

what a coordinated equilibrium would achieve. But that is not to say that this coordinated equilibrium will be characterized by the lower-standard countries in the Nash equilibrium moving upscale, leave aside their duplicating the levels currently in vogue in the United States, for example. Indeed, the economist John Wilson has shown that the world may be characterized even by a race to the top, not to the bottom.[10]

But the real problem is not theoretical. It is simply that we have little evidence that governments actually play the race (choosing to attract investments) by offering to cut standards or that multinational corporations actually are attracted by such concessions and thus are competing in such a race. A great deal of empirical evidence suggests that multinationals do not choose environmentally unfriendly technologies, for example, or even locations because the environmental regulations are less stringent.[11] Moreover, the race to the bottom occurs far more in another space: in tax concessions offered by governments (including local and state governments in federal countries) to attract multinationals. Few governments, certainly now that democracy has broken

[10] See his essay in Bhagwati and Hudec, *Fair Trade and Harmonization*, vol. 1.

[11] This was the burden of Arik Levinson's well-known research, reported in Bhagwati and Hudec, *Fair Trade and Harmonization*, vol. 1. T. N. Srinivasan and I (chap. 4 of Bhagwati and Hudec, vol. 1) offer a number of reasons why multinationals may be indifferent to making an extra buck by playing down to lower standards. A couple of recent studies, for alternative locations in close proximity in the United States, suggest, however, that there is some sensitivity to lower standards in choosing locations by firms.

out worldwide, are likely to say instead to multinationals: come and make profits by polluting our waters and air.[12]

My own view is that, since there is little evidence of multinationals (who add up to the bulk of the direct investments, as distinct from small firms) choosing to exploit lower environmental and labor standards, we should simply extend our key standards (as distinct from wages, of course) to our firms abroad, on a *mandatory* basis: do in Rome as Americans do, not as Romans do.[13] It would assuage the fears of the environmentalists and of those seeking dignity and safety for workers abroad, without imposing serious constraints that these firms do not already impose on themselves (if the evidence is indeed as I have argued above it is).

Alongside this mandatory action, I would also encourage the growth of alternative *voluntary* codes, such as the Social Accountability Label, SA8000, on whose board I have served, and which is now in business with over fifty factories certified in twelve countries.

The mandatory codes will naturally differ across the countries that adopt them since they merely reflect an extension of national codes and laws; the voluntary codes differ among themselves but are identical across countries for ev-

[12] A splendid recent article by Daniel Drezner, "Bottom Feeders," *Foreign Policy* 121 (November–December 2000): 64–70, provides a huge amount of documentation and arguments denying the existence of a race to the bottom. The author concludes: "The race-to-the-bottom hypothesis appears logical. But it is wrong. Indeed, the lack of supporting evidence is startling."

[13] I suggested this in an op-ed article in the *New York Times*, March 24, 1993, reprinted in *A Stream of Windows*.

eryone who signs on to them. Between them, they provide a splendid and more efficient and equitable alternative to the inappropriate demands for countervailing so-called social dumping and for legislation aimed at preventing a hypothetical but nonexistent race to the bottom.

Does Free Trade Damage the Environment?

Let me turn to the concerns of some influential environmentalists, that free trade harms the environment.[14] Here, let me cite again the two central propositions from the postwar theory of distortions and welfare that I stated in the first lecture. For they also bear dramatically on and underline the mistakes underlying the arguments of these critics of free trade. Let me recall them:

PROPOSITION 1.

In the presence of market failure (or distortion), free trade is not necessarily the best policy.

PROPOSITION 2.

(1) Where the distortion is domestic, a domestic (tax-cum-subsidy) policy targeting it will be appropriate and free trade can then be restored as the suitable first-best trade policy; (2) where the distortion is external, free trade must be departed from as part of the suitable first-best policy addressed to the distortion.

[14] I would refer you to two debates I have had with Herman Daly, a leading environmentalist in the United States, in *Scientific American*, reprinted in my essays, *A Stream of Windows*, and with Teddy Goldsmith,

From the viewpoint of the assertions of the ill effects of free trade, or just trade in much popular parlance, on the environment, and the associated concerns that free trade, and the economic prosperity it is supposed to promote, comes at the expense of the environment, these propositions immediately tell you that

- Just as free trade is not necessarily optimal when environmental policy is absent or inadequate (so that we have a market failure), neither is (an arbitrary level of) protection.
- If we put in place an appropriate environmental policy, we get back to free trade as the appropriate trade policy.

The former conclusion extends immediately also to the environmental question: Protection in the presence of market failure in the environment space will not necessarily improve the environment, whereas we will have both environmental[15]

---

the leading environmentalist of the United Kingdom, in the English intellectual magazine *Prospect*, reprinted in *The Wind of the Hundred Days*.

[15] I should state that the best solution need not produce a level of environmental damage that pleases environmentalists if the cost of producing a reduction in such damage exceeds the cost to national income at the margin. By setting the value attached to environmental improvement sufficiently high, this margin can be extended in favor of a higher environmental protection as desired. Thus, the environmentalists in the United States believe that the legislation for clean air and water cannot be subjected to cost-benefit analysis, by which they mean of course that the shadow price of environmental degradation on these two dimensions is set at infinity.

and economic welfare at their efficient best when both an appropriate environmental policy and free trade are in place.[16]

To underline the first point, to convince environmentalists of the first conclusion, the 1992 GATT Annual Report (unfortunately not repeated annually since) on *Trade and the Environment*, directed ably by Richard Blackhurst who was the chief economist at the time, and which I helped write as economic policy adviser to the director general of GATT, produced examples where protection compared to proposed trade liberalization would be worse on the environmental dimension, with environmental regulations in place as they were. One example related to the imposition of voluntary export restrictions on the export of Japanese cars to the United States in 1981. For several reasons that economists have analyzed at length,[17] quantitative restraints will generally shift the composition of exports from a restrained country towards higher-quality items. The economist Robert Feenstra showed that this had happened with

---

[16] Of course, this is strictly speaking true, as proposition 2, part 2, states, for a country without monopoly power in trade or with its firms being in imperfectly competitive product markets. See the discussion in the first lecture.

[17] Among these reasons is that higher quality will be associated with a higher price, and the quotas imply premiums that must be paid equally by an importer of every car. Therefore, the tax or tariff implied by the premium is a larger proportion of the price of lower-quality imports. Hence, the effective tariff rate implied by the quota is higher for lower-quality items, shifting demand at the margin away from them. For a full discussion of alternative theories, see the extended discussion in Bhagwati, Panagariya, and Srinivasan, *Lectures on International Trade*.

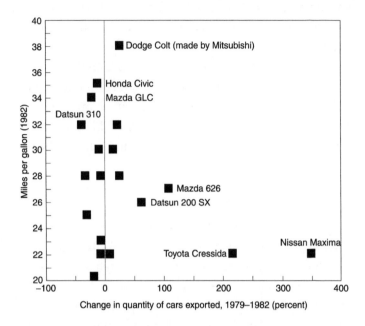

Fig. 1. Gas mileage of cars exported to the United States before and after Japan acquiesced in voluntary export restraints. Perverse consequences for the environment may result from trade restrictions: sales of fuel-efficient models declined, whereas those of gas guzzlers soared. (*Source:* Robert C. Feenstra, University of California, Davis.)

Japanese cars: the Japanese exports had shifted to larger cars that were generally gas-guzzlers, increasing the environmental pollution from car imports. (See figure 1.)[18]

The main example in the report related to agricultural trade liberalization, where the Australian economist Kym

[18] The chart was constructed by Feenstra and has been published by me in *Scientific American*, November 1993, 18–23.

Anderson showed that it would shift production from the EU to the developing countries and therefore increase income in both of them, while *also* improving world environment because the EU agriculture was heavily pesticide-intensive compared to that in the developing countries. Freeing trade was thus a win-win situation for both environmental improvement and income gain: harmony, not discord, was at hand![19]

Of course, free trade does not always do this: examples can be found of environmental damage as the result of the freeing of trade. A recent example is the controversy over shrimp farming in Southeast Asia, which has been accompanied by a tremendous increase in shrimp exports and hence can certainly be attributed to the possibility of trade. Unfortunately, such farming has led to accumulation of dissolved organic matter from metabolites and decomposition of uneaten feeds in the ponds, and dumping of polluted water into surrounding land and waterways, destroying mangroves and damaging soil quality, thus affecting adversely the livelihoods of traditional fishermen and farmers. Although no reliable estimates are available on the extent of such damage, and on whether the gain from shrimp farming is more than offset, or only partially offset, by the spillover losses, it would appear that the former might be likely. Many nongovernmental organizations (NGOs) have argued that this outcome shows that trade is bad and must be bottled up. But that is

---

[19] This is not to say that, at the margin, some developing countries' agriculture is turning today to increased use of pesticides that may damage the environment. It is still nowhere near enough to reverse the Anderson argument.

tantamount to throwing the baby out with the bathwater, because trade is a powerful engine for prosperity and hence social good as well. The correct answer surely is twofold:

• If the spillover was despite prior knowledge—as has turned out to be the case with tobacco companies—then clearly there is a case for award of torts damages, and the laws must be enacted, if not already available, to allow for such action.

• If the spillover is unanticipated and substantial—and this is surely true in many cases, such as the arsenic poisoning in Bangladesh, a tragic result of tubewells installed with UN aid for *clean* water—then that should be occasion for relief and adjustment assistance to the poor among the afflicted, as with disaster relief, while the shrimp-farming industry is then subjected to the polluter pay principle.

Both these prescriptions come from the trade theorists' propositions 1 and 2 outlined above. Where proposition 2 helps out, in particular, is to teach us that, with environmental markets established and the market failure fixed (through enactment and enforcement of the polluter pay principle), we *can* unambiguously get back to free trade. So, in the end, free trade does emerge as the fully appropriate policy (but in tandem with an environmental policy, of course).[20]

And let me emphasize that, while the agricultural example relates to world efficiency and environment, the focus of the

[20] But do not forget what proposition 2 teaches: that, even in the absence of the environmental policy, it may well be the better policy vis-à-vis protectionism!

theoretical analysis is really on what a nation ought to do to achieve the best outcome on trade and on the environment, left to its own choices. That is altogether different from the question as to whether *other* nations trading with it should require that *its* environmental (or, for that matter, its labor) standards and policies should be set differently from what they are.

Advancing Social and Moral Agendas: Free Trade and Appropriate Governance

At the outset of this lecture I did consider that question from the viewpoint of the *self-interest* of these other nations, as expressed in their fair trade arguments. And I shall conclude the lecture by tangentially returning to that theme by examining, and rejecting, the fears of many trade unions that trade with poor countries is driving down the real wages of unskilled workers in the rich countries: for this fear surely prompts many of them to ask for higher standards abroad, since these would presumably raise the cost of production abroad and thereby moderate competition.

This strategic consideration by fearful trade unions is best understood by thinking of a beast charging at you. Either you can try to catch it by its horns, which is the equivalent of *import* protectionism in the context of the rush of international competition, or you may reach behind the beast and hope to catch it by its tail and break its charge, which is the equivalent of raising the foreign rivals' cost of production, or what can be seen as *export* protectionism. The former can also be thought of as *isolationism;* the latter may be called *intrusionism.* It is not surprising in this perspective that the foreign production most closely and systematically targeted by the intrusionists is often labor-intensive, where the rich countries are at a serious competitive advantage, having lost comparative advantage in these industries to the poor countries.

But it would be a mistake to think that it is only self-interest, or what we economists call the egoistical objective, that drives the demands for higher labor and environmental standards elsewhere. So do altruistic reasons. Thus, in regard to child labor for example, NGOs devoted to the subject have no competitiveness interest: they would presumably object to little green men on Mars putting little green children to work even though we had no trade with Mars! Similarly, Human Rights Watch, on whose Academic Advisory Committee (Asia) I serve, objects to China's violation of civil and political rights for its citizens, and protectionist reasons do not cross its mind or taint its agenda. Morality *sans* borders is their motto.

Now if these groups were to use approaches to advancing their agendas that had nothing to do with trade sanctions, either ad hoc or (as is the current practice with rich-country NGOs and their trade unions) by "linkage" to trade treaties and to trade institutions such as the WTO, relying instead on suasion, labeling, private boycotts, and related techniques, there would be little dissension.

But their reliance on trade sanctions as the only technique with "teeth" has caused a deep divide between the proponents of free trade and the advocates of social agendas. I would also contend that this preference ignores the basic lesson of proposition 2, interpreted as implying that, if we wish to advance several objectives, we will generally need an equal number of policy instruments. So both social and moral agendas and trade liberalization cannot be efficiently pursued through one instrument, that is, trade treaties and institutions that subject market access to the fulfillment of a menu of social agendas such as those sought to be put into a Social Clause at the WTO, for instance, by the United States and the European Union. By trying to kill these two birds (i.e. social agendas and freer trade) with one stone (i.e. trade treaties and institutions), you are most likely to miss both. Indeed, we have been doing so, I will seek to show.

I shall also argue that there are added reasons why this principle of economic policy underlines the importance of pursuing different agendas in international agencies suited to the specific agendas for which they were set up: the WTO for trade liberalization, the International Labor Organization for labor standards, the United Nations Environment Program for environmental issues, UNICEF for children's rights, UNESCO for cultural preservation, and so on. None of this is to deny the importance of policy coordination when (and only when) there are necessary interfaces between these agendas.

Missing Two Birds with One Stone

The demands for inclusion of the Social Clause in the WTO have compromised the freeing of trade. This was evident from President Clinton's failure in 1997 to get his fast-track authority renewed by Congress: the Republicans, stronger supporters of free trade than the Democrats, would not

admit social agendas into trade negotiations as requested by
the president, whereas the Democrats were divided into
those who wanted more stringent requirements in the proposed legislation, and the rest. True, several special factors
played a role, including the low credibility of the president
in the quid pro quo promises he was making to win votes,
since he had failed to deliver on such promises following
the NAFTA votes. But the social agenda issue played a principal role.

Then again, the WTO Ministerial in Seattle in November–
December 2000 ended in chaos and a debacle, failing to
launch the anticipated Millennium Round of the first WTO
multilateral trade negotiations. A principal cause again was
the major North-South dissensions over so much as sanc-
tioning a WTO study group on the subject, which major
developing countries saw as an attempt by the United States
to get a foot in the door and then the whole body shortly
thereafter.

So we have been missing one bird: the freeing of trade.
Indeed, there is now real danger that the world will degenerate into a further outbreak of inherently discriminatory
PTAs, while the multilateral trade negotiations (MTN) system of nondiscriminatory trade barrier reductions under
WTO auspices languishes over the North-South battles on
the Social Clause.

But then we are also missing the other bird: the advancing
of the social agenda. One definite result of pushing for labor
(and purely domestic-pollution-related environmental)
standards at the WTO has been the near unanimity of opinion in the developing countries that the real aim of the rich

countries' trade unions and governments is to deter competition—that is, intrusionism. Thus, these demands are widely seen as protectionism hiding behind a moral mask. In short, the moral case is devalued by the context and the means by which it is being pursued. It is therefore seriously compromised and impaired. So we wind up missing the other bird as well.

In fact, the latter point is not just a matter of perception; in my judgment, it is also the real face of what is going on. You see it in the self-protecting and other-directed de facto selectivity of the trade-sanctionable issues that the rich countries want to put into the Social Clause at the WTO. Here, the talk has now shifted to putting into it the "core" labor standards that have been agreed to at UN meetings such as the Social Summit in Copenhagen. But think about the matter a little and you see the calculation behind what is actually being proposed. Not all these core standards are to be taken as matters to be implemented on fast-track. For instance, gender discrimination is not on the fast-track for implementation. If it was, nearly all trade would cease. So where do the rich nations want fast-track rapid-fire action? You guessed it right: on child labor. Why? Because that is where the poor countries can be confidently expected to be the defendants, while the rich nations can equally confidently expect to be the plaintiffs.

Did I hear anyone say that the many sweatshops in the garment district downtown from where I teach in New York, or the much-documented quasi-slavery conditions for migrant labor in American agriculture in Georgia and Mississippi should also be among the issues highlighted for fast-track action in the Social Clause? The silence is deafening.

Recall also the U.S. policy of suspending the entire exports from an industry where only some fraction is subject to a lapse (as in recent actions taken against all shrimp exports from India for nonuse of turtle-excluding devices, when the bulk of the shrimp farming is on farms, not oceans). Explicitly putting these issues on the table for immediate, fast-track implementation would surely put America's textile and agricultural exports at serious risk. So do not expect them to be, no matter the moral talk. Instead, expect action only on those "moral" issues, and within them only on those aspects, where a "side" effect, but most important effect, is the protection of your industries.[21]

None of this cynical exploitation of moral issues for de facto protectionism should be a matter for surprise. After all, trade negotiations and treaties typically relate to competitiveness; and this aspect will dominate whatever the genuine moralists among us want. As George Stigler would have said: the moral issue will be captured by those bothered by competitiveness considerations (and, in this instance, by those that bear particularly on poor-country exports of labor-in-

[21] I might add also that, even on unionization and the rights to bargain collectively and so forth, U.S. policymakers are supremely unaware that their own violations are enormous. These violations of worker's human rights have been splendidly documented in a recent report brought out by Human Rights Watch, *Unfair Advantage: Worker's Freedom of Association in the United States under International Human Rights Standards* (New York: Human Rights Watch, 2000).

tensive products such as textiles and shoes). At a poker game
where men drink whiskey and tell dirty jokes, do not expect
the players to burst into singing madrigals.

Developing Another Stone or Several Pellets: Appropriate Governance

And so I come to the question of an alternative stone, or
even several pellets, to address social agendas. In the present
context, this involves (1) going to an appropriate international agency to do the job; and (2) getting away from trade
sanctions as a way to achieve progress in social agendas. Take,
for instance, the case of workers' rights or core labor standards, focusing on child labor and on the right to organize.

The International Labor Organization is an appropriate
agency to deal with these difficult issues, sorting out their
economics and ethics in light of a vast amount of postwar
experience and thought. It was set up explicitly for that purpose. Its structure and its staff need improvement; but that
is simply a matter of the member countries putting their
shoulder to the wheel and their hands in their wallets.

The WTO has no staff or capability to deal with these
complex issues. Nor will it have them. Its staff is just around
five hundred, whereas the Bretton Woods institutions have
several thousands. The WTO has, at less than ten in its Economics Division, fewer economists than any half-decent
university, whereas the World Bank and the International
Monetary Fund have literally hundreds. The IMF's travel
budget alone exceeds the WTO's entire budget. The World
Bank throws away millions of dollars on conferences, such

as its hugely expensive and recurring ABCDE (Annual Bank Conference on Development Economics) jamboree, last held in Paris—I joke that the conference has made no progress, having been stuck after six years at the first letters of the alphabet. By contrast, when I was economic policy adviser to the director general of GATT, Mr. Arthur Dunkel, it took us forever to find a sum of approximately twenty-five thousand dollars to fund a conference to investigate specific questions relating to the proposed Annual Report on Regionalism.

The starvation of the WTO and the financial indulgence of the Bretton Woods institutions are not fortuitous. The influential Quad powers—the EU, the United States, Japan, and Canada—will resolutely not augment the absurdly lean WTO budget. This, of course, reflects the cynical business of voting. At Bretton Woods institutions, it is weighted. At the WTO, things work by consensus. You do not need to be a profound observer to predict that resources and action will go then to the Bretton Woods institutions. We therefore have the supreme incoherence, some would call it even hypocrisy, of the richest nations asking the WTO to undertake sophisticated studies and to manage a Social Clause while denying the WTO resources to do this or pretty much anything else. Evidently, the WTO then must take on these agendas but rely for their management (under the high-sounding rubric of "policy coordination") on the foreign legion of a (G7-dominated and hence "reliable") leadership and staff at the World Bank or the IMF.[22]

[22] I was therefore somewhat skeptical when my good friend Nicholas Stern, a most distinguished economist and now chief economist at the

If you think that I am exaggerating, let me cite you just one telling example. As regards intellectual property protection (IPP), demanded insistently by the United States and then by other rich countries, most economists believe that having patents at twenty-year length (as put into the WTO) is, from the viewpoint of worldwide efficiency, suboptimal, just as having no patents almost certainly is also. Many also consider it to be a transfer from most of the poor countries to the rich ones and hence as an item that does not belong to the WTO, whose organizing principle should be the inclusion of *mutually gainful* transactions, as indeed noncoercive

---

World Bank, suggested in an interview in the *Financial Times* recently that the World Bank had the expertise on trade questions to do the work for the WTO. The career paths of researchers depend on which institution they belong to and hence reflect, to some degree, the interests that control those institutions. The World Bank is also unlikely to possess the necessary perspectives that the WTO will have. Thus, Stern published recently a fine op-ed, "Open the Rich Markets to Poor Countries' Exports," *International Herald Tribune*, January 25, 2001, condemning rich-country protectionism. But focusing just on that invites, as would be obvious to a trade expert, the poor countries, as many of their spokesmen did at Davos in January 2001, to blame the rich countries and to forget their own protectionism, which is both greater on average in nearly all sectors and arguably the greater factor in damaging their export and their economic performance. (Cf. J. Bhagwati and A. Panagariya, "Wanted: Jubilee 2010 against Protectionism," Council on Foreign Relations, February 2001, typescript. This also appeared as an op-ed article in the *Financial Times*, March 30, 2001.) In short, the World Bank is unlikely to be the place where one can expect fully informed and nuanced leadership on world trade issues. There is no better alternative than building up the WTO's own economics research staff beyond its minuscule levels.

trade is. But the only institution whose staff was allowed to write clearly and skeptically about it at the time of the Uruguay Round was the GATT, whereas the World Bank played along with IPP, even trying to produce reasons why it was good for the poor countries. Even now, despite all the talk about poverty alleviation, the World Bank's staff, research, and aid are being used, I suspect, in a way that, instead of calling into serious doubt the economic logic of intellectual property protection, can be interpreted as contributing to the know-how that will eventually enable rich countries to get poor countries to set up administrative machinery to enforce intellectual property rights for the benefit of the rich countries.[23]

Let me stress that these issues are indeed complex. Only a specialized agency with adequate resources can address them effectively. It must also do this with a sense of symmetry across nations that is a necessity if the moral aspects of these agendas are to be credible.

Thus, expertise is surely necessary to assess properly phenomena such as child labor in the poor countries so that the remedies are appropriate to the problem at hand. For instance, the facile assumption that it is enough to proscribe

[23] Interestingly, while today's NGOs at Seattle were finally accepting the argument against IPP as being beneficial to the poor countries, they were putting the blame at the wrong door. The WTO, which they castigated, was merely (mis)used by the rich countries on IPP. The problem was the rich countries themselves. And among the true culprits in the game, going along with the pretense that IPP was beneficial to the poor countries, was the World Bank management, whose stated objective is to assist the developing countries, not the rich countries.

imports of products made with child labor to eliminate it flies in the face of the fact that less than 5 percent of the output produced by children enters foreign markets. Both economic analysis and empirical observation suggest that trade sanctions may only push children into worse occupations, with female children winding up even in prostitution.[24]

Expertise is also critical to a symmetric treatment of rich and poor nations, as surely required by a proper perspective on human rights. To see this, consider yet another example. While the Democrats in the U.S. Congress typically assume that the violations of workers' human rights occur only in the poor countries, and they gracefully announce that there will be grace periods for the poor countries to come up to snuff before trade sanctions kick in, the reality is that the United States itself is massively in violation of these very rights: a fact that only an informed specialized agency can be expected to document. Let me give you just two quotes (which happen to underline points that I have been making now for some years in arguing against the Social Clause), from the admirable and authoritative recent Report on Workers' Freedom of Association in the United States, brought out just a few months ago by Human Rights Watch (United States):[25]

> Millions of workers are expressly barred from the law's protection of the right to organize. The U.S. legal doctrine

[24] This alternative is not fanciful and appears to have happened in Bangladesh in the textile garments industry, according to an Oxfam study much cited when the Harkin Child Labor Deterrence Act, with trade sanctions, was before the U.S. Congress.

[25] See Human Rights Watch report, *Unfair Advantage*.

allowing employers to permanently replace workers whose
right to strike effectively nullifies the right. Mutual support
among workers and unions recognized in most of the world
as legitimate expressions of solidarity is harshly proscribed
under U.S. law as illegal secondary boycotts.

Many workers who try to form and join trade unions to
bargain with their employers are spied on, harassed, pres-
sured, threatened, suspended, fired or deported or otherwise
victimized in reprisal for their exercise of the right to freedom of association.

A suitably strengthened International Labor Organization
can be charged to produce such informed, impartial, and
authoritative analyses of the various workers' rights issues
in all member countries, just as the WTO under its Trade
Policy Review Mechanism does for trade policy in creating
the necessary knowledge on which many interested groups
can act.[26]

While I do not rule out the use of trade sanctions per se,
and they can be helpful if the violations of human rights
are egregious and widely agreed to be so, in which case a
multilateral embargo can be deployed to advantage,[27] their

[26] There are already the rudiments of such an approach in the annual
review by eminent jurists of the conformity of member countries to rati-
fied conventions at the International Labor Organization. But the model
of the Trade Review Policy Mechanism at the WTO is worth considering
as a supplement that would go a lot towards what I am suggesting in the
lecture.

[27] See my extensive treatment of the subject of trade sanctions for
human rights in my contribution to the Arthur Dunkel festschrift: Bhagwati and Matthew Hirsch, eds., *Uruguay Round and Beyond* (Ann Arbor:
University of Michigan Press; New York: Springer Verlag, 1998).

use in the form of a Social Clause (which automatically implies the possible use of trade sanctions) is hardly efficient compared to the use of non-trade-sanctions approaches, as would be the case at the International Labor Organization. This is best seen in terms of the child labor question. To make a dent on the problem, we need to do "heavy lifting": for example, work with local NGOs, ensure that children go to school when taken off work, and guarantee that the poor parents' incomes do not shrink below the survival line when the children's income disappears. By contrast, the trade sanctions approach, as I have indicated, is likely to be counterproductive (e.g. by pushing children into worse occupations) and therefore, while inspired by good intentions, could well be wicked in its effects. Recall the cliché: the road to hell is paved with good intentions.

In fact, I would make the general point that, today, the use of non-trade-sanctions approaches is for several reasons likely to be more effective than the use of trade sanctions in advancing social and moral agendas. So the common argument that ILO has no teeth, that is, no trade sanctions, is wrong. I would argue that God gave us not just teeth but also a tongue; and a good tongue-lashing, based on evaluations that are credible, impartial, and unbiased, can push a country into better policies through shame, guilt, and the activities of NGOs that act on such findings. Let me elaborate.

Regarding the inappropriateness of trade sanctions: First, the trade sanctions are usually not well targeted to the problem, as with child labor. Second, they generally harden attitudes in the targeted countries: this was the experience with Section 301 actions by the United States against Japan and

India, for instance. Even if a targeted country signs an agreement, the effort put into compliance may be limited. Third, since the sanctions are used by governments that are themselves morally imperfect, the credibility of their actions in behalf of morality is necessarily suspect and breeds cynicism and evasion.

Regarding the appropriateness of non-trade-sanction approaches: By contrast, impartial reviews by the ILO of the policies of member nations in the area covered by the core rights that they have signed on to as aspirations would induce the nations in serious shortfall to move in the right direction. Between such credible reviews, CNN, and the activities of the NGOs, few nations can be expected to remain indifferent to the pressures so generated. Many examples abound of movements by nations in response to such pressures. They are an illustration of what I have called the Dracula effect: expose evil to sunlight and it will shrivel up and die.[28]

Other Applications of the Principle of Two Birds and Two Stones

Multifunctionality of Agriculture

This principle of added stones to deal with added birds applies to a number of other trade issues that afflict the proponents of free trade today; this is also the way to answer the EU trade commissioner, Mr. Pascal Lamy, when he argues,

---

[28] See my book *Protectionism.*

as he did at Seattle, that agriculture is "multifunctional," much as Monsieur Bove, a protectionist by contrast, fuses agriculture and culture to advance *his* agenda.

Many cynics think that Mr. Lamy's talk of multifunctionality is aimed at throwing up a roadblock to agricultural liberalization. This is in keeping with their view that Mr. Lamy's first line of defense is his insistence at Seattle that the new MTN Round include highly contentious issues such as an agreement on investment (which most NGOs and some influential governments will not go along with) and talks that would eventually lead to a Social Clause at the WTO. For such insistence would sabotage the possibility of a new round.

I do not share these views. Let me say, drawing again on the theoretical principles set out in this and the preceding lectures, that there is a simple answer to reasonable concerns about multifunctionality. For we should be able to find and accept suitable policies that promote or protect the other functions of agriculture while freeing trade. Thus, greenery could be subsidized as such, directly rather than indirectly and inefficiently through trade barriers that protect agricultural production in France and the EU generally.

Trade and Culture

The same can be said for the concerns about culture that afflict proponents of free trade. These too can often be addressed more efficiently by policies that avoid protectionism. Thus, the desire to preserve one's cinema is better addressed by subsidies to the local production of movies rather than by restrictions on the showing of foreign films. Such restrictions are increasingly meaningless as VCRs, cassettes, and other means of seeing what you wish to see multiply—this was why the PC, the personal computer, turned out to be a deadly foe of the CP, the Communist Party. But even if they were feasible, they are inferior to production subsidies to local production of cinema: the latter preserve consumer choice, and surely it is good for Renoir to compete with Spielberg![29]

The Fear of the Trade Unions: Threat to Real Wages

In conclusion, let me turn to the fear of the labor unions that free trade depresses the real wages of their unskilled members. Mind you, this fear is expressed with respect to trade with poor countries with abundant labor: underlying it therefore is the famous Stolper-Samuelson theorem, whose critical insight is that if you are importing labor-intensive goods and their relative price falls, then (given the assumptions) the real wage of labor will fall. Since we in the rich countries do import labor-intensive goods from the poor countries, the Stolper-Samuelson theorem becomes a dagger aimed at our unskilled workers' jugular. If, with the redistributive state having lost some of its steam, the market-determined outcomes on income distribution are the final outcomes, free trade becomes the trade unions' nightmare.

I shall proceed to argue that this fear is not justified by the facts. But I must first state for the record that *trade with*

---

[29] I have dealt with this issue at greater length in an essay on trade and culture in *Wind of the Hundred Days.*

poor countries as a source of real wage decline in the rich countries is not the only way in which we can link up trade and wages. I and Vivek Dehejia argued some years ago that *total* trade may depress wages also: if free trade increases volatility of comparative advantage—a phenomenon I have called "kaleidoscopic" comparative advantage with knife-edge properties—then the increased labor turnover could flatten out the earnings curve as firms no longer find it profitable to make investments in firm-level human capital.[30] Then again, my student Elias Dinopoulos and his students and coauthors, in turn, have constructed models where *trade among the rich countries*, using models with interindustry trade, enhances the exploitation of scale economies, increasing the demand for skilled labor and therefore its relative reward. And though they concentrate on the relative wage differential between skilled and unskilled labor, this could, with added assumptions, also generate decline in the *absolute* real wage of the unskilled (which is a separate issue[31] from what happens to unskilled labor's *relative* reward).[32]

---

[30] Cf. Bhagwati and Dehejia, "Freer Trade and Wages of the Unskilled—Is Marx Striking Again?" in *Trade and Wages: Leveling Wages Down?* ed. Bhagwati and Marvin Kosters (Washington, D.C.: American Enterprise Institute, 1994). See also my lead essay in *A Stream of Windows*.

[31] Thus, in the two-by-two Stolper-Samuelson analysis, with specialization, it is easy to construct a case where the wage differential has moved against labor with a decline in the labor-intensive good's relative prices and yet the real wage increases relative to the initial situation.

[32] See, for instance, Elias Dinopoulos and Paul Segerstrom, "A Schumpeterian Model of Protection and Relative Wages," *American Economic Review* 89 (1999): 450–72; Dinopoulos, Constantinos Syropoulos, and Bin Xu, "Intra-industry Trade and Wage Income Inequality," May 2000, Uni-

Needless to say, it is not these alternative linkages between trade and real wages that haunt the unions. For them, it is the specter of competition from the low-wage countries that scares them into multiple reactions that undermine the liberalization of trade with the poor countries. Some wish to roll back earlier trade liberalization (as in NAFTA with Mexico) with the poor countries. Some want a standstill, arguing that free trade should only be with "like-wage" countries, that is, among the rich, high-wage countries (as in CUFTA, between only Canada and the United States). Many others ask for what I have called intrusionism: poor countries can come on board only if they agree to raise their labor and other standards, and hence their production costs, to levels that "equalize" burdens with the high-wage and high-standards countries.

So, we must ask: is there anything to these plausible-sounding fears? These fears are palpable. As the Russian proverb goes, fear has big eyes. And in this instance, it has also the ears of large numbers of politicians (e.g. the Democrats in the United States), partly because of the union vote but also because energetic capture of the public space by the

versity of Florida, typescript; and Fuat Sener, "A Schumpeterian Model of Equilibrium Unemployment and Labor Turnover," May 2000, Union College, Schenectady, New York, typescript. Peter Neary also has an interesting recent paper, "Competition, Trade and Wages," University College, Dublin, June 2000, where a quota removal in oligopolistic industries leads, via encouragement to both foreign and domestic firms to invest more aggressively, to raising their demand for skilled labor and hence increasing the wage differential in favor of skilled workers.

unions and their allies has created a general sense among the people that free trade with the poor countries with low wages and standards is a major problem for our workers.

Let me confine myself to two important arguments, both of which discount these fears greatly. In fact, I will suggest that, instead of hurting real wages of workers, the effect of trade with poor countries is likely to have been even favorable, moderating the decline that would have occurred otherwise from unskilled-labor-saving technical change.

First, going back to the Stolper-Samuelson theorem, the problem is that this argument cannot get off the ground because, during the 1980s when the real wages in the United States fell or their growth decelerated significantly (fig. 2), the relative prices of labor-intensive goods actually seem to have risen![33] Assuming that the main underlying explanation is exogenous to autonomous policy and other changes within the United States itself, we must then explain why the world prices of labor-intensive goods have changed in the direction opposite to what is expected by the unions and other fearful folks. Actually, once you do think about this question, the puzzle is easy to explain.

The reason is that some of the poor nations became rich in the 1980s and steadily moved up what the late Bela Balassa used to call the ladder of comparative advantage: they had become net importers of labor-intensive goods, absorbing the new exports of labor-intensive goods from countries

[33] The same paradox seems to hold for the 1970s, when real wages of U.S. workers kept increasing but the relative prices of labor-intensive goods seem to have fallen, not risen.

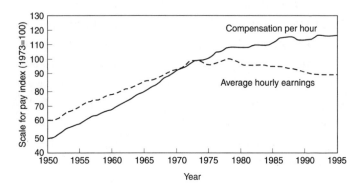

Fig. 2. Real average hourly earnings and compensation in the United States, 1950–95. Figures are adjusted for inflation using CPI-U-XI. Compensation includes wages, salaries, and benefits of employees in the nonfarm business sector. Hourly earnings are for production and nonsupervisory workers in the private nonfarm sector. (*Source:* Bureau of Labor Statistics, Economic Report of the President, 1996; M. Kosters, American Enterprise Institute, May 1996.)

poorer than themselves. This is the story, to some extent, in the 1970s, when Japan's withdrawal from exports of labor-intensive goods absorbed much, but not all, of the exports of the four dynamic newly industrialized countries (NICs): Taiwan, South Korea, Singapore, and Hong Kong. It is an even more significant story in the 1980s, when the offset of China's entry as a major net exporter of labor-intensive exporter is provided by the shift out of such exports by the NICs (fig. 3). Looked at directly in terms of underlying causes, capital accumulation and technical change in the rapidly growing economies have put downward pressure on the production of labor-intensive goods—a conclusion that we know from general-equilibrium analysis of the output-composition changes from these phenomena when we hold goods prices constant—and so the tendency has been to raise, not lower, the world prices of labor-intensive goods.[34]

Second, unions often argue that the outflow of direct foreign investment (DFI) either costs jobs or drives down wages. But surely, whatever the purely economic merits or demerits of this contention, it cannot withstand the fact that, during the 1980s, when the pressure on real wages was the most intense, there was also an almost equal *inflow* of DFI into the United States. In fact, that DFI is a two-way street has been very much on the minds of international economists for nearly four decades; and there is no excuse really for having one's eyes trained only on the outflow.

As always, concretizing this point helps. In their excellent recent book, *The Coming Prosperity*, the *Wall Street Journal* reporters Bob Davis and David Wessel write about a stretch of Interstate 95 going through North Carolina now known as the Autobahn, with several top German multinationals having come in as the region lost textiles factories to foreign locations. The low-paying jobs in textiles have vanished, and

[34] This argument is empirically supported by the work of the Australian economist Ross Garnaut. I have developed the argument more fully in my latest paper on the problem, "Play It Again Sam: Yet Another Look at Trade and Wages," in *Essays in Honor of T. N. Srinivasan*, ed. Gus Ranis and Laxmi Raut (Amsterdam: Elsevier, 1999). This paper is also reprinted in *The Wind of the Hundred Days*.

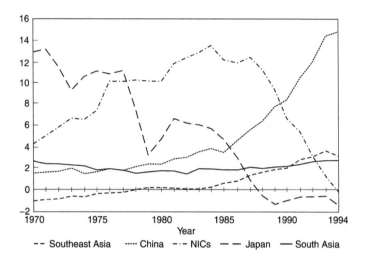

Fig. 3. Net exports as a percentage of world imports of labor-intensive manufactures, East and South Asia, 1970–94. Southeast Asia includes the ASEAN countries (including Vietnam); the NICs are Taiwan, Hong Kong, Korea, and Singapore; South Asia includes India, Pakistan, Bangladesh, and Sri Lanka. (*Source:* UN trade data, International Economic DataBank, Australian National University, prepared by Ross Garnaut.)

the workers have wound up getting paid far more at Siemens and other German firms. They are now rooting for globalization, for investment and trade in the global economy.

Perhaps I should also recall how, during a BBC debate where I and Martin Wolf of the *Financial Times* were pitted against two irate opponents working with NGOs, the producer played a tape of the French mayor of the town that was losing its Hoover factory to England. The justifiably unhappy mayor was fulminating against multinationals that disappeared to cheaper and better locations. I pointed out that I doubted if his predecessor had complained when Hoover, an American firm, had come to France in the first place! In short, DFI gets the boot when it goes out and the red carpet when it comes in; but the public often hears only the complaints, and the unions and politicians do not take the balanced, net view of the matter that is required.

So, for these and other reasons that I must urge you to read for yourselves, I believe that the alarm of the unions over the adverse effects of free trade on the real wages of workers in the rich countries is far from persuasive.

Free Trade and Poverty in Poor Countries

Also unpersuasive is the frequent complaint in some *poor* countries that free trade accentuates poverty. Speaking at least for India, I would say that autarky helped produce a slow average growth rate of 3.5 percent annually for over a quarter of a century until early 1980s. During this period, it was virtually impossible to pull people up into gainful employment, and out of poverty, in a significant way. With the 1980s, the increasing pace of outward-oriented reforms has been associated with growth rates closer to 6–6.5 percent annually; and, after much controversy, there is a fair degree of consensus that poverty has been dented. Contradicting the anti-free-trade rhetoric that flows ceaselessly from the street theater and even from certain international agencies, the facts show that a shift out of autarky into closer integration into the world economy is producing better, not worse,

results for poverty reduction. Free trade proponents have
little to worry about on that score.

None of this, of course, is to deny the relevance of several
policy observations, grounded again in what we know from
theory.

• The optimal speed at which one liberalizes is not
necessarily the fastest. Shock therapy (i.e., going ahead
at full throttle) has been advocated by economists such
as Jeffrey Sachs, who argued that "you do not cross a
chasm in two leaps" (to which Padma Desai had the
devastating riposte: "You do not cross a chasm in one
leap either, unless you are Indiana Jones; you drop a
bridge"). Both political factors and economic factors
such as rigidity of labor markets determine the optimal
speed.

• While the central tendency is for freer trade to
dominate less free trade in creating prosperity, there
are bound to be occasional downsides: in this instance,
poverty may be accentuated. Clearly then we need adjustment assistance programs to take care of these adverse effects when they arise. Again, to reject freer trade
because of occasional adverse effects is to hurt your
cause of reducing poverty.

• In some poor countries, the ability to provide such
adjustment assistance, which requires budgetary support, may be strictly circumscribed. In that case, it
should be precisely the role of Bretton Woods agencies
to provide grant funds to make possible a welfare-enhancing, poverty-reducing transition to free trade.

Getting to Free Trade: Alternative Approaches and Their Theoretical Rationale

Alternative Approaches to Freeing Trade

Aggressive Unilateralism

Conventional Unilateralism: Going Alone

Preferential Trade Agreements: Regionalism and Bilateralism versus Multilateralism

Concluding Remark

In the first lecture, I considered the many influential challenges to free trade that have arisen in the last 150 years and showed how the dramatic, indeed revolutionary, developments in the postwar theory of commercial policy had met these enduring challenges head on and put the case for free trade on a firm footing. In the second lecture, I argued that, while the new challenges of today were different, they too could be surmounted, many by using the very same theoretical principles of the modern theory of commercial policy.

I would boldly say therefore that we can confidently instruct our policymakers, and tell our students, that free trade is a policy that makes eminent sense. But then the different question arises, on which also there is much controversy today: *how do we get to free trade?* For there are alternative approaches to liberalizing trade, and the ones that appeal most to the policymakers are not necessarily the ones that make most economic sense. Indeed, in some cases (such as the widespread and growing use of preferential trade agreements) it is pretty clear that something like Gresham's law has operated, with bad approaches driving out the good ones. Evidently, we cannot sheath our analytical swords: new battles await us.

Alternative Approaches to Freeing Trade

There are basically four different ways in which trade is being freed in the world today, two having to deal with *unilateral* approaches and the other two with *reciprocal* bargaining. The unilateral method embraces

- Aggressive unilateralism: the pursuit, often with threats, of unilateral reductions in *others'* trade barriers (as with the Section 301 methods of the American legislators)[1]
- Conventional unilateralism: reduction of *one's own* barriers

The reciprocal reduction of trade barriers, on the other hand, consists in demanding a quid pro quo: I shall not reduce my barriers unless you do so simultaneously. Such insistence on *reciprocity* is typically at the heart of multilateral trade negotiations under GATT, and now WTO, auspices (though, for years, the poor countries were exempt from it under the dispensation of what came to be known as Special and Differential Treatment). This manner of reducing barriers I have called *first-difference* reciprocity. Reciprocity is of the essence, also, when preferential trade agreements (PTAs) such as free trade agreements and customs unions, sanctioned by Article 24 of the GATT, are signed: everyone agrees then to final and total freeing of within-PTA trade; that is, all member countries are fully free of trade barriers vis-à-vis one another. This is *total*, or full, reciprocity.[2] So we have essentially two classic forms of reciprocal reduction of trade barriers:

- Reciprocity in multilateral trade negotiations under GATT/WTO auspices

---

[1] The phrase "aggressive unilateralism" was introduced by me in *World Trading System at Risk*; and it was the subject of extensive analysis in Bhagwati and Patrick, *Aggressive Unilateralism*.

[2] See my discussion in *World Trading System at Risk*.

- Reciprocity in preferential trade agreements

I will now address the merits and demerits, the nuances and the broad implications, of these alternative approaches. If I may confess to my conclusions, to give you a glimpse tantalizing enough to gain your attention but not so much as to lose your attendance, I shall argue that both conventional unilateralism and MTN reciprocity have a useful role to play in freeing trade, whereas both aggressive unilateralism and PTAs are a pox on the world trading system.

Aggressive Unilateralism

It is clear enough that only powerful nations can extract trade concessions unilaterally from others by threats, whether in the form of trade retaliation or war or by other means. Hegemonic powers with illiberal regimes have been known to impose their will on, and extract concessions by force from, their trading partners. No one ever accused the Communist superpower, the Soviet Union, of attempting anything except one-way gains from its trading partners in East Europe.

But how does the United States, a liberal hegemon that, except for serious blemishes in its South American record, has been an empire "by invitation" and an empire "by example," extract unilaterally determined trade concessions under the threat of retaliation? For that is exactly what Section 301 legislation aimed to do; and that is exactly what the actions taken by the United States Trade Representative under its authority actually do.

Evidently, the answer must lie in a legitimating conviction that the United States was unfairly open while its trading partners were closed. Thus, the conventional practice that you either reduced your own trade barriers unilaterally, or that you balanced trade concessions in first-difference reciprocity, was set aside by the United States, which opted instead to require that the other countries make unilateral concessions on the ground that only then would the United States achieve full reciprocity, that is, a correction of the asymmetrically greater American openness that its postwar generous and unbalanced concessions had created.

The reality, however, had little to do with the rhetoric and the self-delusion that accompanied and fueled the drive for aggressive unilateralism. Thus, the past history of trade negotiations revealed one central truth: the United States had always insisted on reciprocity in trade concessions, rarely giving away unmatched concessions because it would have had great difficulty passing them through Congress.[3] It was hardly to be expected that the United States would then be so far unbalanced in its relative openness. Besides, its contention that Japan was closed while the United States was open, and therefore that unilateral demands could be made on Japan to change its trade barriers and practices under

[3] The only major exception is provided by the first three postwar GATT rounds of multilateral trade negotiations, all within six months of each other, when Japan and much of Europe lay vanquished and their economies in shambles.

threats of retaliation, made little sense in face of the over-whelming economic evidence against it.[4]

In the end, Section 301 has played itself out. It had two central provisions. First, it provided for retaliatory action for nonful-fillment of other countries' obligations already embodied in trade treaties; and second, it had provisions for extracting new concessions under threats of tariff retaliation for what the United States had determined unilaterally to be unreasonable.

The former grew out of the frustration that, even when the United States had won rulings at the GATT, the blocking of the decision by the losing party from adoption by the General Council often nullified that victory. Now that a rul-ing stands at the WTO as binding unless the successful party chooses to abandon it, the reason for unilateral retaliation for blocked decisions has disappeared. The latter, on the other hand, has turned out to attract so much opprobrium worldwide—who, after all, likes a bully?—that the United States has in effect abandoned that particular, obnoxious version of 301 actions. Besides, the latest ruling by WTO on 301 has virtually signed its death warrant.[5]

So the era of aggressive unilateralism, specific as it was to a superpower, has come to an end, though the unique

---

[4] Much of this was the subject of writings by Douglas Irwin, Gary Sax-onhouse, and myself. My own writings have been largely reprinted in my essays, *A Stream of Windows.*

[5] For the decision that effectively put an end to the use of Section 301 to extract new concessions unilaterally, as distinct from seeking to enforce compliance with concessions agreed to under previous trade treaties and

combination of might and self-righteousness that leads to unilateral actions by the United States continues to plague much else in trade policy today, as in the unilateral assertions of the ability to exclude products made by processes and production methods that the Congress deems offensive.[6]

Conventional Unilateralism: Going Alone

Most trade economists have long been wedded to unilateralism as the correct way to think about freeing trade. They have regarded the reciprocal bargaining away of trade barriers as surrender to a "mercantilist" way of thinking.

I recall Harry Johnson saying precisely this, in reference to reciprocal reductions of trade barriers at the GATT rounds of negotiations, when I was in his class at Cambridge in 1954; and he certainly put it down somewhere since he rarely let a thought go to waste unwritten.[7] Why did Johnson

found wanting by GATT, see the Panel Report, December 22, 1999, WTO/DS152/R.

[6] I did not have the time to address this latter issue when dealing with the trade and environment issue in the second Lecture. The question of how best to deal with "values-related" objections to foreign processes and production methods is an intricate issue that I and many others have written about extensively. Again, see chapters 1 and 4, in particular, in Bhagwati and Hudec, *Fair Trade and Harmonization*, volume 1, and also my Anita and Robert Summers Lecture at Wharton School, reprinted as chapter 7, *The Wind of the Hundred Days*.

[7] But, given his prodigious output—once Charles Kindleberger teased him in a review of his collected writings that Harry reminded him of an ad for a purgative in his youth: "it works while you sleep"—I have found

consider reciprocity to be a mercantilist phenomenon? His reasoning was simple. While economic theory argued that it was good for one to free trade unilaterally, trade negotiators always behaved as if one's trade liberalization was a concession—a sentiment that could be aptly characterized as mercantilist—that had to be matched reciprocally by other countries' trade liberalization.

True, Johnson had in mind the negotiators in Geneva at the GATT, and the successive rounds of reciprocally negotiated tariff cuts since the Second World War. The economists Kyle Bagwell and Robert Staiger, who have done remarkable research on the GATT's principles, call the practice "GATT-think." But that is a mistake, I believe, since insistence on reciprocity of *some* kind is inevitable when there is a trade *negotiation* that is bilateral, plurilateral, or multilateral, so that *GATT-think* needs to be changed to *negotiators-think*, of which the negotiators at GATT or now the WTO are only one example.

---

it difficult to find a specific written reference to this castigation of reciprocity as mercantilism. It is like looking for a needle in a haystack.

Indeed, I might recall that, since he joined Chicago after Cambridge and Manchester, his colleague there, George Stigler, an economist with acerbic wit, often regaled their common friends by recalling how a journalist had come by asking how many articles each professor had written. When Stigler mentioned a modest number, the journalist exclaimed: "But there is this far younger professor down the corridor, Harry Johnson, who says he has written several hundred." Stigler told him : "Ah, but mine are all different"! And that was before the personal computer made us all Johnsonesque in responding to the many demands on our time to write for conferences and volumes.

Should we then go along with this Johnsonesque view of
the matter, putting unilateralism a virtuous step ahead of
reciprocity as a way of liberalizing trade? Let me say at the
outset that the answer for trade liberalization is a more sub-
tle and nuanced one. It can be capsuled in three propositions, additional to the two I introduced in the first lecture.

PROPOSITION 3
*Go alone (that is, cut trade barriers unilaterally) if others
will not go with you.*

PROPOSITION 4
*If others go simultaneously with you (i.e., there is
reciprocity in reducing trade barriers), that is still better.*

PROPOSITION 5
*If you must go alone, others may follow suit later:
unilateralism then leads to sequential reciprocity.*

Let me elaborate on these propositions analytically and
then offer some empirical observations in support of the
case for unilateralism, for (simultaneous) reciprocity, and
for unilateralism leading to "sequential" reciprocity.

Proposition 3: Go Alone If Others Do Not Go with You

The classic statement of the case for going alone if others
will not go with you is, of course, by my Cambridge teacher,
Joan Robinson, who was gifted with a talent for saying things
both plainly and wittily. You will recall that she famously

remarked once that if others throw rocks into their harbor, that is no reason to throw rocks into your own. This is worth remembering, as it is a lesson that often gets lost in public debates: and the reason is, of course, the obsession with "fairness" that I discussed in the previous lecture. Many wrongly think that it is unfair if one's market is open and one's rival's is not: a mistake that many make today as they contemplate rich-country protectionism and then claim that therefore it is unfair to ask poor countries to reduce barriers.[8]

In short, we need to remember that if we refuse to reduce our trade barriers just because others do not reduce theirs, we lose from our trading partners' barriers and then lose again from our own.[9] In many ways, when Prime Minister Robert Peel repealed the Corn Laws unilaterally in 1846 to usher in free trade in Britain, he showed that he had learned this lesson, having been exasperated with the refusal of con-

---

[8] Cf. Bhagwati and Panagariya, "Wanted," which has also appeared as an op-ed in the *Financial Times*, March 30, 2001.

[9] We must, of course, add the usual riders when there is national monopoly power in trade. Thus, unilateral trade liberalization is beneficial only if the optimal tariff is zero (i.e., there is no national monopoly power in trade) or when the reduction in barriers is from a level above the optimal tariff and does not go so far below the optimal tariff as to actually bring a welfare loss. Similar qualifications are necessary when firm-level imperfect competition exists, as discussed in the first lecture. A proper incorporation of these arguments in a formal discussion of the case of unilateralism *versus* reciprocity is in my long introduction to J. Bhagwati, ed., *Going Alone: The Case for Relaxed Reciprocity in Freeing Trade*, forthcoming from MIT Press in 2002.

tinental powers to pursue trade liberalization in the reciprocal framework implied by the then-fashionable bilateral
trade treaties.[10]

Proposition 4: If Others Go with You, That Is Still Better

For the same reason, we can argue that if others do liberalize
in return for one's trade liberalization, then we gain twice
over. This is, of course, broadly true. The formal argumentation for it can be tricky but is readily doable.

Thus, imagine that we have what, following Bagwell and
Staiger, I call a reciprocal trade liberalization that preserves
the external terms of trade where they were in the previous
higher-tariff equilibrium. This will necessarily increase the
welfare of both countries. Why? Because, with terms of trade
unchanged, and with tariffs having declined in both countries, each country will have only production and consump-
tion gains from the reduced tariff! It is then easy to see
that, compared to unilateral trade liberalization, such terms-
of-trade-preserving reciprocal trade liberalization will be
productive of greater gains for each country. This is a neat
theorem; it also puts a formal structure on the intuition
that reciprocal trade liberalization will lead necessarily to
greater gain.[11]

---

[10] As I note later, however, Peel also believed that "sequential" reciprocity would likely follow.

[11] See Bhagwati, *Going Alone*.

What can we say about bargaining so as to achieve this reciprocity (which may, however, not materialize, as Peel believed had happened with earlier efforts to get European countries to go to free trade alongside Britain through bilateral treaties)? Evidently, it makes sense and is not "mercantilist," though there *is* a danger that excessive use of the language of concessions in trade bargaining can lead, and has indeed led, to a widespread bureaucratic and political acceptance of the wrongheaded view that import liberalization is expensive rather than gainful and must be offset by concessions for one's exports. This, in turn, has fed the popular protectionist misconception that trade is good but imports are bad! Evidently, such a viewpoint does create difficulties for trade liberalization: as George Orwell would have reminded us, language matters. And as we scholars believe, sloppy arguments have a tendency to come back at us: we may win battles that way but may lose the war.

Let me then suggest at least one other way in which reciprocity may be helpful.[12] In a pluralistic system, it may help a government mobilize export-oriented lobbies who would profit from expanding foreign markets to countervail the import-competing lobbies that profit instead from reducing trade. True, as trade economists well understand, one's reduced protection itself creates incentives for exporters: protectionism implies a bias against exports. But one may be

---

[12] I advanced four different arguments in defense of reciprocity, of which this lecture considers only two, in considering the issue in my introductory essay in Bhagwati and Patrick, *Aggressive Unilateralism*.

forgiven for assuming, quite correctly, that this benefit is not easily perceived by the exporters who would benefit (indirectly) from such a change. What reciprocal trade liberalization does is to add to, in a perfectly direct and hence salient fashion, the incentives of exporters and hence to facilitate, through use of countervailing power, the reduction of one's own trade barriers.[13]

Proposition 5: If You Go Alone, Others May Liberalize Later

Then we get to the interesting proposition that if others do not see the light and wish to go on with their protectionism, we might be able to get them to follow us with a lag. So we get in effect sequential reciprocity. This thought is not entirely new: it had occurred to Prime Minister Peel for sure. Indeed, he argued that Britain's success with the unilateral introduction of free trade would set an example and should induce the recalcitrant nations to follow suit.[14]

---

[13] The distinction between direct (hence visible and salient) and indirect effects of reforms is extremely important in discussing the political economy of reform. I am afraid this point is not fully understood by social scientists such as Robert Bates, whose work on reforms in African agriculture aggregates the two types of reforms to arrive at "net" incentives that typically signify nothing. Get me a peasant who will passively accept the withdrawal of a subsidy on his fertilizers because a change in the exchange rate will make agriculture more profitable sufficiently to outweigh the loss of subsidy (and that too, based on Bates's or the World Bank's model)!

[14] His views have been extensively documented in my book *Protectionism.* Also see the brilliant article by Douglas Irwin, "Political Economy

The matter is best seen, as always, in terms of supply and demand: in this instance, of protection. The supply of protection in foreign nations can shrink if, as Peel believed, the success of unilateral free trade by a country seduces them into imitating the reasons for this success. But the demand for protection abroad may also shrink: a possibility that Peel did not allow for but that I have argued for and some of my students have modeled ably.[15] This happens essentially through the fact that the expansion of trade (thanks to the unilateral trade liberalization elsewhere) can strengthen the export lobbies relative to the import-competing lobbies: in jargon, the political-economy equilibrium in foreign nations is shifted in favor of those who seek reduced rather than increased protection.

Let me add briefly that the empirical reality shows extensive resort to unilateral trade liberalization in the last two decades in Eastern Europe, in Latin America (especially Chile), in Asia (especially in Australia, New Zealand, and Indonesia, and since 1991 in India as well), and yet earlier in Singapore and Hong Kong. There is also evidence of it

and Peel's Repeal of the Corn Laws," *Economics and Politics* 1, no. 1 (1989): 41–59.

[15] See Rodney Ludema and Daniel E. Coates, "A Theory of Unilateralism and Reciprocity in Trade Policy," Georgetown University Working Paper 97-23, March 1989; and Pravin Krishna and Devashish Mitra, "A Theory of Unilateralism and Reciprocity in Trade Policy," Brown University Department of Economics Working Paper 99/09, April 1999. The models used by these authors are quite different, but they both demonstrate how the demand for protection abroad can get affected by one's own tariff liberalization.

in the highly innovative financial and telecommunications sectors in the United States, with some evidence of sequential reciprocity by the European Union and Japan (both moving to respond with their own liberalization in light of American example and success at competition when earlier they refused to do so under reciprocity and even Section 301 threats).[16]

Preferential Trade Agreements: Regionalism and Bilateralism versus Multilateralism

That brings me to the classic choice between two different forms of reciprocal trade liberalization: preferential trade liberalization and nondiscriminatory (i.e. most-favored nation, MFN) trade liberalization. Interestingly, the original GATT agreement embraces both. MFN is the most important rule in GATT, just as the "freedom to associate" (i.e. to organize trade unions) is the holiest of workers' rights at the International Labor Organization. Equally, in Article 24, the architects of the GATT allowed for free trade areas and customs unions (the latter going beyond the former to a common external tariff), both being preferential trade agreements (PTAs).[17] The GATT has also, over time, permitted developing countries a greater latitude to undertake

[16] See my introductory chapter 1 in Bhagwati, *Going Alone*.

[17] These are admissible under constraints that, in practice, have never been used to challenge successfully any PTA in history. There are other exceptions to MFN, as with antidumping duties and Article 20 provisions on public safety, that are permissible as well. But they are not relevant to the issue in the text.

PTAs that fall short of free trade areas and customs unions: the latter two require a commitment to getting internal tariff barriers down to zero, whereas the former permit permanent discrimination at levels other than zero.[18]

However, as the great economist Jacob Viner pointed out in 1950, when asked by the Carnegie Commission to write a report on postwar commercial arrangements, free trade areas (FTAs) are not free trade. While they remove tariffs for member countries, they also increase the handicap (for any given external tariff) that nonmembers suffer vis-à-vis member-country producers in the markets of the member countries, implying therefore protection against them. So, FTAs are two-faced: they free trade and they retreat into protection, simultaneously. Of course, those who are used to sound bites and cannot think of more than two words at the same time will read *free trade area* as *free trade*! So, since clearly the phrase *FTA* is calculated to confuse it with free trade, I have urged over the years, with some success, that economists call FTAs by the phrase *PTAs*, which, at minimum, alerts the public and the politicians to the fact that here we have another species.

Trade Diversion

Indeed, as soon as we recognize this fact, we arrive at Viner's startling and profound insight: FTAs can actually worsen the welfare of member countries, even worsen worldwide effi-

---

[18] For different GATT provisions under which PTAs can be established, see chapter 1 in Bhagwati, Pravin Krishna, and Panagariya, eds., *Trade Blocs: Alternative Analytical Approaches* (Cambridge: MIT Press, 2000).

ciency. The reason is what he called *trade diversion*. By making market access less burdened by tariffs for a member country, one may cease importing from a lower-cost nonmember source. For instance, U.S. access to Mexico's market becomes tariff-free under NAFTA, but Japan's is not, so Mexico shifts from cheaper imports from Japan to more expensive imports from the United States. In that case, there is clearly a loss that may (or may not) be offset by the gain that consumers derive from the lower prices *they* pay and from the fact that some higher-cost domestic production may also be reduced as domestic prices fall and move closer to the cheapest prices in world markets.

Viner thus threw a spanner in the works for those who believed that any move, even preferential, towards free trade was welfare-improving. As we see the frantic rush to form ever more PTAs, this lesson is clearly forgotten and the erroneous pre-Vinerian intuition has returned to center stage. It has been aided also by unsupportable arguments in favor of such an "unarchitectural" and technically regressive approach, embracing all forms of trade liberalization as equally good, by economists of the enormous caliber of former U.S. Treasury secretary Larry Summers, who has argued that trade diversion is a distraction best discarded from policy debate.[19]

In fact, the Summers prescription has been unwittingly taken to heart by economists who these days analyze the effects of PTAs as if Viner had never existed, treating all trade expansion among member countries of a PTA as if it were simply welfare-improving trade creation (as it would be under nondiscriminatory MFN trade liberalization). This was true of the report on the effects of NAFTA that was produced by the well-known consulting firm Data Resources, which dutifully collected the data on Mexico's imports from the United States and celebrated the fact that they had moved up dramatically despite Mexico's significant reduction in total imports thanks to the November 1994 peso crisis and its aftermath, wholly forgetting to say that this seemed to be precisely the kind of trade diversion (at Mexican expense) that Viner had taught us to think about.[20] In fact, Arvind Panagariya has made a rough-and-ready calculation that suggests that the Mexican loss from trade diversion could be as large as $3 billion annually.

Then again, Alexander Yeats, at the World Bank, made a plausible calculation of a significant loss from trade diversion in Mercosur—the customs union among Brazil, Argentina, Uruguay, and Paraguay—causing an uproar in Brazil because the Brazilian diplomats thought that this was a plot by NAFTA, where the hegemonic power is the United States, to discredit Mercosur, where the hegemonic power is Brazil.[21] In fact, an important lesson from that episode, and

---

[20] NAFTA meant that the trade barriers against the United States were reduced on schedule, whereas Mexico raised, because of the peso crisis, 504 external tariffs, taking advantage of bindings in excess of the actual tariff levels. Thus, there was a double whammy against nonmembers of NAFTA.

[21] These studies, and other aspects of the trade diversion issue, are discussed more fully in chapter 1 in Bhagwati, Krishna, and Panagariya, *Trade Blocs*.

the current discord between Brazil and others on the dimensions and pace of implementation of a Free Trade Agreement
of the Americas that masks the underlying battle for hegemony between the United States and Brazil, is that regional
trade agreements inevitably politicize trade more than
multilateral trade agreements do.

Perhaps the most serious way in which PTAs risk trade
diversion is through the tendency to accommodate enhanced post-PTA competition from a member of the PTA,
not by reducing one's own uneconomic, high-cost production, but by raising barriers against more efficient nonmembers and reducing their exports to oneself. Thus, assume that
Mexico starts crowding the United States after NAFTA has
taken hold and U.S. trade barriers have come down. If the
high-cost U.S. production declines and Mexico's low-cost
production expands, that is obviously good: it is what Viner
would have called *trade creation*, a phrase that is appropriate
in suggesting welfare enhancement. But suppose that, in
place of this outcome, we have American producers scream-
ing for help and that the United States authorities raise nontrade barriers against Taiwan, the least-cost producer and
supplier. Then the imports from Taiwan are replaced by
higher-cost imports from Mexico, while the highest-cost
U.S. production is maintained. So the trade creation (i.e.,
shift of production from the United States to Mexico) that
would have taken place is replaced by trade diversion (i.e.,
shift of production from Taiwan to Mexico) instead. The
culprit, of course, is the raising of trade barriers, *after* the
PTA between Mexico and the United States is formed,
against Taiwan, the nonmember of the PTA. In short, we

have a raising of external trade barriers (vis-à-vis nonmembers) that is endogenous to the formation of the PTA.[22]

Of course, Article 24 of the GATT that sanctions PTAs also prohibits the raising of external tariffs and import quotas. But such increase in trade restrictions against nonmembers can still happen through the use of elastic and selective nontariff barriers such as the use of antidumping actions and voluntary export restraints, which can be targeted, virtually at any level, at specific countries.[23] And these are precisely the forms of protectionism that have become fashionable, making the safeguards built into Article 24 ineffective.

Besides, if the tariffs against nonmembers are bound at the GATT/WTO at levels higher than the ones in force, that also leaves a member country free to raise even the external tariffs despite Article 24 once the PTA has been in operation: an example being the raising of Mexican external tariffs on 504 items, while the tariffs against items from NAFTA sources were left untouched, during the 1994 peso crisis.

---

[22] This possibility of trade creation being replaced by trade diversion through the endogeneity of the external trade barriers has been formally shown by me and Panagariya in chapter 1 of Bhagwati, Krishna, and Panagariya, *Trade Blocs.*

[23] It is precisely the fact that antidumping actions can be used selectively against, not just countries, but specific firms, and that dumping margins are often calculated arbitrarily through "reconstructed" costs and even prices, that has made them the preferred method of protectionism. Voluntary export restraints share similar properties, though the Uruguay Round has brought them under control (with results that are not quite as intended since, in the nature of the case, they reflect implicit understandings that can escape effective proscription).

Spaghetti Bowl: A Systemic Problem

Trade diversion in particular PTAs is worry enough. But today, it has only a minor part in the play. The villain is the systemic problem posed by an explosive proliferation of PTAs.

This situation was not foreseen by the architects of GATT Article 24. Indeed, they would be aghast today at the wild horses and rogue elephants that have marched through the door that the article (and a couple of later enabling clauses) opened to preferences. An increasing number of PTAs of all kinds have been formed. By the last count, there were over four hundred formed and contemplated; and the number was growing by the week. I have little doubt that if this epidemic had been foreseen at the end of the Second World War, the architects of the GATT would have had serious reservations about inserting Article 24 into the agreement.[24]

Looking at this explosion when the number of PTAs was yet barely in three digits, I remarked that the situation was turning into a "spaghetti bowl": a messy maze of preferences as PTAs formed between two countries, with each having bilaterals with other and different countries, the latter in turn bonding with yet others, each in turn having different rules of origin (as required by the preferences sought to be

---

[24] Of course, Article 24 itself has been seriously emasculated, or its teeth pulled, in its working. It is fair to say that many of its requirements have been effectively bypassed, with virtually no proposed PTA having ever failed to receive GATT authorization.

given and taken, without "leaks" to nonmembers via entry into members) for different sectors,[25] and so on. I called it a spaghetti bowl because it is an unruly mass of criss-crossing strings that, in any case, is beyond my capabilities. (Once I used this metaphor in an after-dinner speech on PTAs and the world trading system. I noticed the chairman's puzzlement in place of the amused grin that I expected; and then I realized that, of course, he was an Italian for whom eating spaghetti posed no challenge.)

Lest you think I exaggerate, let me turn your attention to figures 4 and 5, one on the spaghetti bowl in Europe, the other in Africa. By the time these lectures get into print, these charts will have been overlaid by yet more PTAs, showing a still denser and crazier criss-crossing of bilaterals and plurilaterals. These are misleadingly called *regionals* by many—but tell me, what is regional when Singapore or Israel goes with the United States?

So we have a definite systemic problem. Viner's worry over trade diversion, not a product of fevered imagination as Larry Summers would have it, but the result of an acute and profound intelligence, pales in comparison with the damage that the PTAs now impose on the world trading system, overwhelming multilateralism and its central tenet

---

[25] Rules of origin are required to ensure that only production in member countries enjoys the PTA preferences. Thus, for instance, if Canada has a lower tariff on diesel engines than the United States, Japanese diesel engines could enter Canada with a lower tariff and then enter the United States at a zero tariff under NAFTA, unless there was a "rule of origin" preventing this

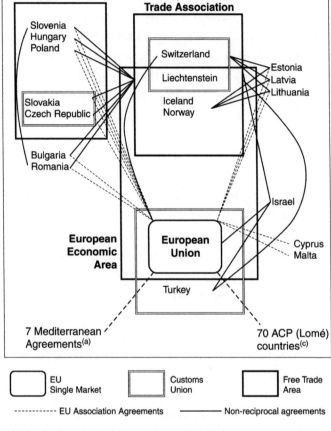

Fig. 4. The European spaghetti bowl; prepared by
Arvind Panagariya, University of Maryland.

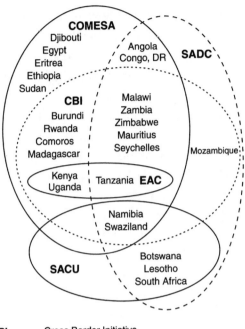

CBI	Cross Border Initiative
COMESA	Common Market for Eastern and Southern Africa
EAC	Commision for East African Co-operation
SADC	Southern African Development Community
SACU	Southern African Customs Union

Fig. 5. The African spaghetti bowl; prepared by
Arvind Panagariya, University of Maryland.

of nondiscrimination. I must ask why these bilaterals and plurilaterals have multiplied beyond anyone's imagination. There are many reasons, several political.

Some of the cynical, but certainly not altogether fanciful, reasons for the observed preference for preferential trade liberalization under bilaterals and plurilaterals are these:

- Bureaucrats get posh jobs. Take the beautiful drive leading from the airport to downtown Montevideo in Uruguay and you can see the building that will house the Mercosur secretariat, the counterpart of the powerful European Commission. Often, the bureaucrats in charge get the rank of ambassadors.

- At multilateral negotiations, the media often concentrate on such big players as the European Union's trade commissioner or the U.S. trade representative. But at bilaterals, the media give attention to the local politicians and bureaucrats, who therefore have a personal stake in proliferating their pet PTAs. This is best described therefore as the CNN theory of the spaghetti bowl: CNN makes the bowl ever bigger.

- Bureaucrats and politicians are rarely in an architectural mode, and few really understand the distinction between FTAs and FT (free trade). Their short tenure also predisposes them towards immediate results; and bilaterals are easier to sign. So they opt for more bilaterals.

In fact, the tendency to equate all kinds of trade agreements in the political sphere reached such absurd proportions during the Clinton administration that U.S. Trade Representative Mickey Kantor dismissed all such distinctions and asserted in a classic public declaration that he was interested "in results, not theology." I also heard him compliment a bureaucrat for having participated in the negotiation of over three hundred trade agreements, of which two were the Uruguay Round and NAFTA, and the rest were trade-restricting textile bilaterals under the long-standing multifiber agreement (MFA), a notorious piece of protectionism!

But the truly compelling reason these PTAs have prolifer-
ated is simply what we economists call the (Nash) pursuit
of individual interest in an uncoordinated fashion when
there is a superior coordinated pursuit of a better solution.
As bilaterals multiply, countries begin to feel that they are
being frozen out of markets within those bilaterals.[26] They
then begin plotting their own, going with politically pliable
partners. So more bilaterals are started. And pretty soon we
have the phenomenon we see today: an escalating expansion
of bilaterals.[27]

We are thus reproducing in the world trading system, in
the name of free trade but through free trade areas that
spread discrimination against producers in nonmember nations, the chaos that was created in the 1930s through similar
uncoordinated pursuit of protectionism that discriminated
in favor of domestic producers. In both cases, the preferred
solution would have been nondiscriminatory pursuit of freer
trade.

Trade Minister Alec Erwin of South Africa has pointed to
yet another downside of this outbreak: the poorer countries
are least able to manage a trading system riddled by complex
preferences and rules of origin.

---

[26] Thus, Business Roundtable, an influential U.S. lobby of businessmen,
recently expressed alarm over the U.S. businesses being left out of world's
fragmenting markets and asked the U.S. government to pursue more PTAs
of its own. Similar alarms have been expressed in India, Australia, and
indeed several countries, by their governments and/or their business
groups.

[27] Cf. my article "A Costly Pursuit of Free Trade," *Financial Times*,
March 6, 2001, and a letter to the editor, "Trade Blocked," in the *Econo*

As these bilaterals multiply, my concerned friends say, the bowl is overflowing. The spaghetti bowl is now perhaps an inadequate metaphor. Australian ambassador to the WTO Geoff Raby says: the pesto sauce in the spaghetti has now been replaced by diesel oil, the cheese by nuts and bolts.

PTAs and the Multilateral Freeing of Trade

Even if most observers now deplore the systemic chaos, can we still harbor the hope that PTAs are only part of a dynamic process, defining a time-path, that leads towards the shared goal of multilateral free trade? As I put it a decade ago in the 1990 Harry Johnson Lecture in London, are bilaterals building blocks for free trade, or stumbling blocks?

This question came up especially when the United States, which had avoided PTAs and exclusively favored multilateral trade negotiations and treaties, abandoned that position in the early 1980s and began a policy of embracing PTAs under Article 24. The rationale then was that at the November 1982 GATT Ministerial, Europeans refused to start a new round to reduce trade barriers. The huge protectionist threat in Congress forced the hand of the Reagan administration, which opened a regional PTA trade initiative with Canada. The United States decided that, since there was no driving the multilateral highway, it could only travel by walking the regional, preferential country road. So the decision was

---

mist, March 3–9, 2001, on the causes and consequences of the explosion of bilaterals.

made to walk on two legs: one temporarily asleep in Geneva at the GATT, the other active in the PTA framework.

What has happened since, as I have already documented, is that instead of walking on two legs, we have wound up on all fours. Many of the different bilaterals today bear little resemblance to one another: each has features that reflect the politics and the economic circumstance of the pair of countries in question. As the Japanese vice minister for finance said in Davos in January 2001, "We in Japan have finally been forced into pursuing bilateral agreements to free trade, but we must admit to a genuine worry that, in terms of Professor Bhagwati's language of building and stumbling blocks, the bilateral agreements worldwide are blocks of varying size and shape. It is hard to see how they can be used to build multilateral free trade."[28]

Concluding Remark

In my view, the current world trading system is at a cross-roads. While the case for free trade is robust, having surmounted the traditional objections over two centuries, and is capable of meeting the recent objections from civil society and labor unions as well, the headlong rush into preferential trade has left free trade in a sorry state. It is as if we were

---

[28] For the growing theoretical literature on the political-economy-theoretic models that try to analyze the incentives to expand or limit membership in PTAs, see the extensive review in the introduction to Bhagwati, Krishna, and Panagariya, *Trade Blocs.* The most interesting such work is by Richard Baldwin, Pravin Krishna, and Philip Levy.

finally convinced that exercise was good for our health, but had nevertheless surrendered to lassitude and sloth. I am a sufficient optimist to think that such folly cannot persist. Perhaps these lectures will provide intellectual ammunition that will help those who seek the necessary change in course. I certainly hope so.

Index